STILL STEAMING

Britain's Heritage Standard-Gauge Railways 2025-2026

EDITOR
John Robinson

Twenty-sixth Edition

FOREWORD & ACKNOWLEDGEMENTS

We were greatly impressed by the friendly and cooperative manner of the staff and helpers of the railways which we selected to appear in this book, and wish to thank them for the help they have given. In addition we wish to thank Bob Budd (cover design) and Jonathan James who has provided us with photographs for several railways.

There are a number of other standard-gauge heritage railways that are currently being developed and we hope to be able to include some of these in future editions of Still Steaming.

In addition to the Heritage Railways itemised, we have provided the details of our magnificent National Railway Museum, its sister site, Locomotion along with other museums, all of which are well worth a visit.

Although we believe that the information contained in this publication is accurate at the time of going to press, we, and the Railways and Museums itemised, are unable to accept liability for any loss, damage, distress or injury suffered as a result of any inaccuracies. Furthermore, we and the Railways are unable to guarantee operating and opening times which may be subject to cancellation without notice.

If you feel we should include other locations or information in future editions, please let us know so that we may give them consideration. We would like to thank you for buying this guide and wish you 'Happy Steaming'!

John Robinson

EDITOR

British Library Cataloguing in Publication Data
A catalogue record for this book is available from the British Library

ISBN-13: 978-1-86223-537-3

Copyright © 2025, SOCCER BOOKS LIMITED. (01472 696226)
72 St. Peter's Avenue, Cleethorpes, N.E. Lincolnshire, DN35 8HU, England

All rights are reserved. No part of this publication may be reproduced, stored in a retrieval system or transmitted, in any form or by any means, electronic, mechanical, photocopying, recording, or otherwise, without the prior written permission of Soccer Books Limited.

Printed in the UK by 4edge Ltd

COVER PICTURE

The cover image shows GWR 5526 leaving with a WLS Special from Buckfastleigh Station at the South Devon Railway on 28th September 2024.

CONTENTS

Foreword & Acknowledgments 2
Contents 3-4
Alderney Railway 5
Aln Valley Railway 6
Appleby Frodingham Railway 7
Avon Valley Railway 8
Barrow Hill Roundhouse Railway Centre 9
The Battlefield Line 10
Beamish – The Living Museum of the North 11
The Bluebell Railway 12
Bodmin & Wenford Railway 13
Bo'ness & Kinneil Railway 14
Bowes Railway 15
Bressingham Steam Museum 16
Bristol Harbour Railway 17
Buckinghamshire Railway Centre 18
Caledonian Railway 19
Cambrian Heritage Railways 20
Chasewater Railway (The Colliery Line) 21
Chinnor & Princes Risborough Railway 22
Cholsey & Wallingford Railway 23
Churnet Valley Railway 24
Colne Valley Railway 25
Crewe Heritage Centre 26
Dartmouth Steam Railway & River Boat Company 27
Dean Forest Railway 28
Derwent Valley Light Railway (The Blackberry Line) 29
Didcot Railway Centre 30
Doon Valley Railway 31
East Anglian Railway Museum 32
East Kent Light Railway 33
East Lancashire Railway 34
East Somerset Railway 35
Ecclesbourne Valley Railway 36
Eden Valley Railway 37
Embsay & Bolton Abbey Steam Railway 38
Epping & Ongar Railway 39
Foxfield Steam Railway 40
Gloucestershire Warwickshire Railway 41
Great Central Railway 42
Great Central Railway (Nottingham) 43
Gwili Railway 44

3

Helston Railway	45
Isle of Wight Steam Railway	46
Keighley & Worth Valley Railway	47
The Keith & Dufftown Railway	48
Kent & East Sussex Railway	49
Lakeside & Haverthwaite Railway	50
The Lavender Line	51
Lincolnshire Wolds Railway	52
Llangollen Railway	53
Mangapps Railway Museum	54
The Middleton Railway	55
Mid-Hants Railway (The Watercress Line)	56
Mid-Norfolk Railway	57
Mid-Suffolk Light Railway Museum	58
Midland Railway – Butterley	59
Mountsorrel Railway Museum	60
Nene Valley Railway	61
North Norfolk Railway	62
North Yorkshire Moors Railway	63
Northampton & Lamport Railway	64
Northants. Ironstone Railway Trust	65
Peak Rail PLC	66
Plym Valley Railway	67
Pontypool & Blaenavon Railway	68
Ribble Steam Railway	69
Rocks By Rail – The Living Ironstone Museum	70
Royal Deeside Railway	71
Rushden Transport Museum & Railway	72
Severn Valley Railway	73
Somerset & Dorset Railway	74
South Devon Railway	75
Spa Valley Railway	76
Stainmore Railway	77
Stephenson Steam Railway	78
The Strathspey Railway	79
Swanage Railway	80
Swindon & Cricklade Railway	81
Tanfield Railway	82
Telford Steam Railway	83
Tyseley Locomotive Works Visitor Centre	84
Weardale Railway	85
Wensleydale Railway	86
West Somerset Railway	87
Whitwell & Reepham Railway	88
Yeovil Railway Centre	89
Yorkshire Wolds Railway	90
National Railway Museum – York	91
Locomotion	92
Steam – Museum of the Great Western Railway	93
Hopetown – Darlington	94
Manchester Museum of Science and Industry	95
Whitehead Railway Museum	96

ALDERNEY RAILWAY

Address: P.O. Box 75, Alderney, Channel Islands GY9 3DA
Telephone Nº: 07911 739572
Year Formed: 1978
Location of Line: Braye Road to Mannez Quarry, Alderney
Length of Line: 2 miles

Nº of Steam Locos: 1 (not in use)
Nº of Other Locos: 2
Approx Nº of Visitors P.A.: 2,000+
Gauge: Standard and 7¼ inch
Website: www.alderneyrailway.gg
E-mail: alderneyrailway@suremail.gg

GENERAL INFORMATION

Nearest Mainline Station: Not applicable
Nearest Bus Station: Not applicable
Car Parking: Available on site
Coach Parking: Available on site
Souvenir Shop(s): Yes
Food & Drinks: None at the Railway itself but available nearby

SPECIAL INFORMATION

The original line was built during the 1840s to assist in the construction of the large breakwater in Braye Harbour and fortifications on the island. The line itself opened in 1847 and was the first nationalised railway run by the Admiralty.

OPERATING INFORMATION

Opening Times: Easter Sunday then every Saturday from 3rd May until 13th September 2025. A Santa Special operates on Sunday 21st December at 1.00pm and 2.30pm. Please contact the railway for further information. Trains usually run at 2.00pm and 3.30pm although Santa Specials run as shown above.
Steam Working: None at present
Prices: Adult Return £10.00
  Child Return £5.00

Detailed Directions:
The Railway is situated adjacent to Braye Harbour.

ALN VALLEY RAILWAY

Address: Lionheart Station, Lionheart Enterprise Park, Alnwick NE66 2EZ
Information Line Nº: 0300 030-3311
Year Formed: 1995
Location: Alnwick to Greenrigg Bridge
Length: 2,130 metres (almost 1½ miles)

Nº of Steam Locos: 3
Nº of Other Locos: 3 (Diesel)
Approx Nº of Visitors P.A.: 13,500
Gauge: Standard and 7¼ inch
Website: www.alnvalleyrailway.co.uk

GENERAL INFORMATION

Nearest Mainline Station: Alnmouth (5 miles)
Nearest Bus Station: Alnwick (1½ miles)
Car Parking: Available on site
Coach Parking: Available
Souvenir Shop(s): Yes
Food & Drinks: Available at the Buffet Stop Cafe

SPECIAL INFORMATION

The Aln Valley Railway Trust plans to re-open, in stages, the former Alnwick to Almouth branch line, primarily as a heritage railway attraction. The line currently runs from Alnwick Lionheart Station, over the seven-arch Cawledge Viaduct, to a new halt at Greenrigg Bridge where there are toilet and refreshment facilities in a B.G. carriage.

OPERATING INFORMATION

Opening Times: Weekends & Bank Holidays from Easter to September then Halloween Weekend and Santa Specials between Christmas & New Year. Trains run from 11.00am to 3.00pm. A diesel Pacer service runs on Wednesdays in school holidays.
Prices: Adult £10.00
Child £4.50
Under-3s are admitted free of charge except on special events days.
Note: Prices shown above are for Steam and Diesel days. Cheaper return tickets are also available for Pacer Days.

Detailed Directions by Car:
Exit the A1 at Willowburn Junction (just to the south of Alnwick) and follow the brown tourist signs marked "Aln Valley Railway" through the Enterprise Park to Lionheart Station. (SatNav users select NE66 2HT) Buses to and from Alnwick Bus Station (services 472 and X15) stop by the Willowburn Filling Station/Sainsbury's store just to the north of the A1. Follow the brown tourist signs on foot from here for the railway.

Appleby Frodingham Railway

Address: Appleby Frodingham Railway c/o PO Box 1, Scunthorpe DN16 1BP
SatNav: Set destination as DN16 1XA
Year Formed: 1990
Location of Line: British Steel, Scunthorpe
Length of Line: 15 miles used on tours from almost 100 miles of track

Nº of Steam Locos: 5
Nº of Other Locos: 3
Nº of Members: 60
Gauge: Standard
Website: www.afrps.co.uk

GENERAL INFORMATION

Nearest Mainline Station: Scunthorpe (1 mile)
Nearest Bus Station: Scunthorpe (½ mile)
Car Parking: Large free car park at the site
Coach Parking: At the site
Souvenir Shop(s): Yes – at the Loco Shed
Food & Drinks: Available at the Loco Shed

SPECIAL INFORMATION

The Society operates 15 mile Rail and Brake Van tours of the Scunthorpe steelworks site (which covers almost 12 square miles) using its extensive internal railway system.

OPERATING INFORMATION

Opening Times: 2025 Dates: Steam Tours run on: 26th April; 24th & 31st May; 7th June; 12th & 19th July; 23rd August; 6th & 20th September and 4th October. Diesel Tours run on: 5th April; 3rd May; 4th & 28th June; 5th July; 16th August and 11th October.
Note: Please check the website for details of additional tours. Tours must be pre-booked via the website using the 'Book Now' ticket source.
Steam Working: See above
Prices: £25.00 per person (Steam)
£20.00 per person (Diesel)

Detailed Directions by Car:
Exit the M180 at Junction 4 and take the A18 into Scunthorpe. Turn right at the roundabout by Morrisons supermarket and follow Brigg Road for approximately ½ mile. Turn right into Gate E. Car parking is available on the left and the path to the station is on the right.   SatNav users please enter: DN16 1XA

AVON VALLEY RAILWAY

Address: Bitton Station, Bath Road, Bitton, Bristol BS30 6HD
Telephone Nº: (0117) 932-5538
Year Formed: 1973
Location of Line: Midway between Bristol and Bath on A431
Length of Line: 3 miles

Nº of Steam Locos: 6
Nº of Other Locos: 5
Approx Nº of Visitors P.A.: 80,000
Gauge: Standard
Website: www.avonvalleyrailway.org
E-mail: info@avonvalleyrailway.org

GENERAL INFORMATION

Nearest Mainline Station: Keynsham (1½ miles)
Nearest Bus Station: Bristol or Bath (7 miles)
Car Parking: Available at Bitton Station
Coach Parking: Available at Bitton Station
Souvenir Shop(s): Yes
Food & Drinks: Yes

SPECIAL INFORMATION

The line originally opened in 1869 as a direct route from Birmingham to the south coast but was axed in the 1960s following the Beeching Report. Three miles of track has now been re-laid along the Bristol to Bath section of the line.

OPERATING INFORMATION

Opening Times: 2025 dates: Every Saturday, Sunday and Bank Holiday Monday from 29th March to 28th September plus Sundays in October. Open 10.30am to 5.00pm.
Please check the website for further details.
Steam Working: Sundays and Bank Holidays
Prices: Adult £11.00
Concessions £10.00
Child £7.00 (Under-5s ride for free)
Note: Special event tickets should be pre-booked.

Detailed Directions by Car:
From All Parts: Exit the M4 at Junction 18. Follow the A46 towards Bath and at the junction with the A420 turn right towards Bristol. At Bridge Yate turn left onto the A4175 and continue until you reach the A431. Turn right and Bitton Station is 100 yards on the right.

BARROW HILL ROUNDHOUSE RAILWAY CENTRE

Address: Barrow Hill Roundhouse, Campbell Drive, Barrow Hill, Staveley, Chesterfield   S43 2PR
Telephone Nº: (01246) 472450
Year Formed: 1998
Location: Staveley, near Chesterfield
Length of Line: ¾ mile

Nº of Steam Locos: 12
Nº of Other Locos: Over 40
Approx Nº of Visitors P.A.: 30,000
Gauge: Standard
Website: www.barrowhill.org
E-mail: enquiries@barrowhill.org

GENERAL INFORMATION

Nearest Mainline Station: Chesterfield (3½ miles)
Nearest Bus Station: Chesterfield (3 miles)
Car Parking: Space available for 300 cars
Coach Parking: Available
Souvenir Shop(s): Yes
Food & Drinks: Yes – Café

SPECIAL INFORMATION

Built in 1870, Britain's last remaining operational railway roundhouse provides storage and repair facilities for standard gauge steam, diesel and electric locomotives and now also houses a museum and a café.

OPERATING INFORMATION

Opening Times: 2025 dates: Every weekend from 1st March until 7th December from 10.00am to 4.00pm. Please check the centre's website for further information and details of special events.
Steam Working: See above.
Prices: Adults £9.00
    Children £7.00 (Under-5s Free)
    Family Tickets £28.00 (2 adult + 3 child)
Note: Prices may be higher on Special Events days. Please check the website for full details.
Entry to the cafe and shop is free of charge

Detailed Directions by Car:
Exit the M1 at Junction 30 and take the A619 to Staveley (about 3½ miles). Pass through Staveley, turn right at Troughbrook Road. Continue along for ½ mile, pass under the railway bridge and take the turn immediately on the right. Turn left onto Campbell Drive and the Roundhouse is on the left. The railway is signposted with Brown Tourist signs.

THE BATTLEFIELD LINE

Address: The Battlefield Line, Shackerstone Station, Shackerstone, Leicestershire   CV13 6NW
Telephone Nº: (01827) 880754
Year Formed: 1968
Location of Line: The line runs through Market Bosworth

Length of Line: 5 miles
Nº of Steam Locos: 5
Nº of Other Locos: 20
Approx Nº of Visitors P.A.: 60,000
Gauge: Standard
Website: www.battlefieldline.co.uk
E-mail: info@.battlefieldline.co.uk

GENERAL INFORMATION

Nearest Mainline Station: Nuneaton or Hinckley (both 12 miles)
Nearest Bus Station: Hinckley (for Market Bosworth)
Car Parking: Ample free parking available
Coach Parking: At Market Bosworth Station
Souvenir Shop(s): At Shackerstone Station
Food & Drinks: Yes – Buffets available at all stations

SPECIAL INFORMATION

Travel from the Grade II listed Shackerstone Station through the beautiful Leicestershire countryside with views of the adjoining Ashby Canal. Arrive at the award-winning Shenton Station and explore Bosworth Battlefield (1485) before making the return journey.

OPERATING INFORMATION

Operating Info: 2025 dates: Weekends and Bank Holidays from 22nd March to 26th October plus Wednesdays from 23rd July to 10th September, Tuesdays in August and Tuesdays & Wednesdays from 21st to 29th October. Santa Specials operate on weekends in December.
Please check the website for further details.
Opening Times: 11.00am to 4.15pm
Steam Working: From 11.15am to 4.15pm during high season and 11.00am to 3.30pm at other times.
Prices: Adult Return £15.00
Concession Return £10.00
Child Return £10.00 (Ages 3 to 15)
Family Ticket £40.00 (2 adult + 3 child)
Prices shown allow all-day travel but fares for Special Events may be higher.

Detailed Directions by Car:
Follow the brown tourist signs from the A444 or A447 heading towards the market town of Market Bosworth. Continue towards the villages of Congerstone & Shackerstone and finally to Shackerstone Station. Access is only available via the Old Trackbed. (SATNAV - CV13 0BS for car park)

BEAMISH, THE LIVING MUSEUM OF THE NORTH

Address: Beamish, The Living Museum of the North, Beamish DH9 0RG
Telephone N°: (0191) 370-4000 (weekdays) 9.00am to 2.00pm)
Year Formed: 1970
Length of Line: ½ mile

N° of Steam Locos: 15
N° of Other Locos: 2
Approx N° of Visitors P.A.: 765,000
Website: www.beamish.org.uk
E-mail: museum@beamish.org.uk
Gauge: Standard & others

GENERAL INFORMATION

Nearest Mainline Station: Newcastle Central (8 miles); Durham City (12 miles)
Nearest Bus Station: Newcastle (8 miles); Durham (12 miles)
Car Parking: Free parking for 2,000 cars
Coach Parking: Free parking for 40 coaches
Souvenir Shop(s): Yes
Food & Drinks: Yes – a self service tea room, licensed period Public House, Coffee shop and a coal-fired Fish & Chip shop!

SPECIAL INFORMATION

A replica of William Hedley's famous 1813 locomotive "Puffing Billy" steams on the Pockerley Waggonway at Beamish alongside replicas of Locomotion and the Steam Elephant. Heritage Trams also operate on the Beamish Tramway.

OPERATING INFORMATION

Opening Times: 2025: Daily from 31st March to 24th October 10.00am to 5.00pm.
Steam Working: Daily during the Summer months.
Prices: Adult £27.95
              Child £17.25 (Ages 5-16)
              Senior Citizen £21.25
              Family Tickets £47.50 to £78.25
              (price depends on family numbers)
Children under-5 are admitted free.
All tickets allow unlimited free return visits for 12 months except for Evening events.

Detailed Directions by Car:
From North & South: Follow the A1(M) to Junction 63 (Chester-le-street) and then take A693 for 4 miles towards Stanley; From North-West: Take the A68 south to Castleside near Consett and follow the signs on the A692 and A693 via Stanley. (SATNAV DH9 0RG)

The Bluebell Railway

Address: The Bluebell Railway, Sheffield Park Station, near Uckfield TN22 3QL
Telephone Nº: (01825) 720800
Year Formed: 1959
Location: Sheffield Park to East Grinstead
Length of Line: 11 miles

Nº of Steam Locos: Over 30 with up to 3 in operation on any given day
Nº of Other Locos: 4
Approx Nº of Visitors P.A.: 140,000
Gauge: Standard
Website: www.bluebell-railway.com
E-mail: enquiries@bluebell-railway.com

GENERAL INFORMATION

Nearest Mainline Station: East Grinstead (2 minute walk)
Nearest Bus Station: East Grinstead
Car Parking: Parking is available at Sheffield Park and Horsted Keynes Stations.
Coach Parking: Sheffield Park is best for coaches
Souvenir Shop(s): Yes – at Sheffield Park Station
Food & Drinks: Yes – buffets and licensed bars & restaurant

SPECIAL INFORMATION

The Railway runs 'Golden Arrow' dining trains on most Saturday evenings and Sunday lunchtimes. There is also a museum at Sheffield Park Station.

OPERATING INFORMATION

Opening Times: 2025 dates: Open 10.30am to 5.30pm daily (except on Fridays) from 29th March to 27th May and most Thursdays to Sundays in June. Open daily during July and August.
Please check the website for information about later months including Santa Specials in December. Details will become available later in the year.
Steam Working: As above
Prices: Adult Rover From £30.00
Child Rover From £15.00 (Ages 3-15)
Family Rover From £78.00
Note: The prices shown above are for tickets purchased on the day. Discounted prices are available for advance bookings.

Detailed Directions by Car:
Sheffield Park Station is situated on the A275 Wych Cross to Lewes road. Horsted Keynes Station is signposted from the B2028 Lingfield to Haywards Heath road.

BODMIN & WENFORD RAILWAY

Address: Bodmin General Station, Losthwithiel Road, Bodmin, Cornwall PL31 1AQ
Telephone Nº: (01208) 73555
Location of Line: Bodmin Parkway to Boscarne Junction, via Bodmin General
Length of Line: 6½ miles

Nº of Steam Locos: 11
Nº of Other Locos: 9
Year Formed: 1984
Approx Nº of Visitors P.A.: 62,000
Gauge: Standard
Website: www.bodminrailway.co.uk
E-mail: enquiries@bodminrailway.co.uk

GENERAL INFORMATION

Nearest Mainline Station: Bodmin Parkway (there is a cross platform interchange with the Bodmin & Wenford Railway)
Car Parking: Free parking at Bodmin General
Coach Parking: Free parking at Bodmin General
Souvenir Shop(s): Yes
Food & Drinks: Yes

SPECIAL INFORMATION

The Railway has steep gradients and through tickets to "Bodmin & Wenford Railway" are available from all Mainline stations.

OPERATING INFORMATION

Opening Times: 2025 dates: Open most days except Mondays, Fridays and some Saturdays from 1st April to 2nd November then daily in August except Fridays. Open 10.00am to 5.00pm.
Note: Santa Specials run on weekends in December. Please contact the railway for further details.
Steam Working: Most trains are steam-hauled but please check the website for Diesel running days. Daily steam throughout August.
Prices: Adult All-line £23.50
  Concessions All-line £22.50
  Children £12.50 (Under-3s ride free)
  Family Tickets £52.00 to £64.00
    (dependent on numbers in the family)

Detailed Directions by Car:
From the A30/A38/A389 follow the signs to Bodmin Town Centre then follow the brown tourist signs showing the steam engine logo to the Steam Railway on the B3268 Losthwithiel Road.

Bo'ness & Kinneil Railway

Address: Bo'ness Station, Union Street, Bo'ness, West Lothian EH51 9AQ
Telephone Nº: (01506) 822298
Year Opened: 1981
Location of Line: Bo'ness to Manuel
Length of Line: 5 miles

Nº of Steam Locos: 26
Nº of Other Locos: 25
Approx Nº of Visitors P.A.: 70,000
Gauge: Standard
Website: www.bkrailway.co.uk
E-mail: enquiries.railway@srps.org.uk

GENERAL INFORMATION

Nearest Mainline Station: Linlithgow (3 miles)
Nearest Bus Station: Bo'ness (¼ mile)
Car Parking: Free parking at Bo'ness Station
Coach Parking: Free parking at Bo'ness Station
Souvenir Shop(s): Yes
Food & Drinks: Yes

SPECIAL INFORMATION

In addition to the ten-mile journey, passengers should visit Scotland's largest railway museum at Bo'ness Station. The Railway and Museum are operated by volunteers from The Scottish Railway Preservation Society.

OPERATING INFORMATION

Opening Times: 2025 dates: Weekends and Tuesdays from 1st April to 26th October inclusive. Also open Wednesdays in July & August and for Santa Specials in December. The museum is open daily from 1st April to 26th October.
Steam Working: On standard service days, 10.45am, 12.10pm and 2.10pm. The 3.35pm service may be diesel-hauled at weekends.
Prices: Adult Day Ticket £17.00
    Child Day Ticket £10.00
    Family Ticket £48.00 (2 adult + 3 child)
    Compartment Ticket £75.00
        (up to six people per compartment)
Note: Under-5s are admitted free of charge. Higher fares may apply on Special Event Days.

Detailed Directions by Car:
From Edinburgh: Take the M9 and exit at Junction 3. Then take the A904 to Bo'ness; From Glasgow: Take the M80 to M876 and then M9 (South). Exit at Junction 5 and take A904 to Bo'ness; From the North: Take M9 (South), exit at Junction 5, then take A904 to Bo'ness; From Fife: Leave the A90 after the Forth Bridge, then take A904 to Bo'ness.

Bowes Railway

Address: Bowes Railway, Springwell Road, Gateshead, Tyne & Wear NE9 7QJ
Telephone N°: 0785-0916484
Year Formed: 1976
Location of Line: Springwell Village
Length of Line: 1¼ miles

N° of Steam Locos: 2
N° of Other Locos: 5
Approx N° of Visitors P.A.: 5,000
Gauge: Standard
Website: www.bowesrailway.uk

GENERAL INFORMATION

Nearest Mainline Station: Newcastle Central (3 miles)
Nearest Bus Station: Gateshead Interchange (2 miles)
Car Parking: Free parking at site
Coach Parking: Free parking at site
Souvenir Shop(s): Open Thursday to Saturday throughout the year
Food & Drinks: Available

SPECIAL INFORMATION

Designed by George Stephenson and opened in 1826, the Railway is a scheduled Ancient Monument which operated unique preserved standard gauge rope-hauled inclines and steam hauled passenger trains.

OPERATING INFORMATION

Opening Times: The Springwell site is open for pre-booked 90-minute tours on Tuesdays & Thursdays at 10.00am or 1.00pm.
Steam Working: None at present
Prices: Adults £5.00
Children £3.00 (Ages 5 to 16 years)

Detailed Directions by Car:
From A1 (Northbound): Follow the A194(M) to the Tyne Tunnel and turn left at the sign for Springwell.
From A1 (Southbound): Take the turn off left for the B1288 to Springwell and Wrekenton.

BRESSINGHAM STEAM MUSEUM

Address: Bressingham Steam Museum, Low Road, Bressingham, Diss IP22 2AA
Telephone Nº: (01379) 686900
Year Formed: Mid 1950's
Location of Line: Bressingham, Near Diss
Length of Line: 5 miles in total (4 lines)

Nº of Steam Locos: 6 Standard gauge plus many others
Approx Nº of Visitors P.A.: 80,000+
Gauge: Standard, 2 foot, 10¼ inches and 15 inches
Website: www.bressingham.co.uk
E-mail: info@bressingham.co.uk

GENERAL INFORMATION

Nearest Mainline Station: Diss (2½ miles)
Nearest Bus Station: Bressingham (1¼ miles)
Car Parking: Free parking for 100 cars available
Coach Parking: Free parking for 3 coaches
Souvenir Shop(s): Yes
Food & Drinks: Yes

SPECIAL INFORMATION

In addition to Steam locomotives, Bressingham has a large selection of steam traction engines, fixed steam engines plus Dad's Army Exhibits and 17 acres of gardens.

OPERATING INFORMATION

Opening Times: 2025 dates: Daily from 27th March to 2nd November. Open from 10.30am to 5.00pm.
Steam Working: Every operating day except for Mondays and Tuesdays outside the school holidays. Please contact the Museum for further details.
Prices: Adult £19.75
Child £13.00 (Under-3s ride free)
Note: Reduced entry charges are available for visitors who do not take railway rides.
The prices shown above include a Gift Aid donation and online bookings are 50p cheaper.

Detailed Directions by Car:
From All Parts: Take the A11 to Thetford and then follow the A1066 towards Diss for Bressingham. The Museum is signposted by the brown tourist signs. SATNAV please use the following post code: IP22 2AA

Bristol Harbour Railway

Address: Princes Wharf, Wapping Road, Bristol BS1 4RN
Telephone Nº: (0117) 352-6600
Year Formed: 1978
Location of Line: South side of the Floating Harbour

Length of Line: Just under 1 mile
Nº of Steam Locos: 2
Nº of Other Locos: 1
Gauge: Standard
Website: bristolmuseums.org.uk/m-shed

GENERAL INFORMATION

Nearest Mainline Station: Bristol Temple Meads (1 mile)
Nearest Bus Station: City Centre (½ mile)
Car Parking: Pay & Display adjacent to M Shed
Coach Parking: Pay & Display adjacent
Souvenir Shop(s): In the M Shed Museum
Food & Drinks: Café in the Museum

SPECIAL INFORMATION

The M Shed museum opened in June 2011 and has since attracted over 1 million visitors.
Trains run alongside the harbour to link M Shed with the SS Great Britain on the dockside and from M Shed to Ashton Bridge along the New Cut, giving a choice of scenery on alternate routes.

OPERATING INFORMATION

Opening Times: 2025 dates: The M Shed is open daily throughout the year (except on Mondays), but the railway only operates on most weekends from Easter to September.
Please contact the railway for further information. Trains run from 11.00am to 4.00pm.
Steam Working: Every operating day.
Prices: Singles £3.00
         M Shed to Vauxhall Bridge Return £4.50
Note: Children under the age of 6 travel for free.

Detailed Directions by Car:
From All Parts: Follow signs to Bristol City Centre and then the Brown Tourist signs for the Museum. A good landmark to look out for are the 4 huge quayside cranes.

17

BUCKINGHAMSHIRE RAILWAY CENTRE

Address: Quainton Road Station, Quainton, Aylesbury, Bucks. HP22 4BY
Telephone Nº: (01296) 655720
Year Formed: 1969
Location of Line: At Quainton on the old Metropolitan/Great Central Line
Length of Line: 2 × ½ mile demo tracks

Nº of Steam Locos: 30
Nº of Other Locos: 6
Approx Nº of Visitors P.A.: 35,000
Gauge: Standard (also a Miniature line)
Website: www.bucksrailcentre.org
E-mail: office@bucksrailcentre.org

GENERAL INFORMATION
Nearest Mainline Station: Aylesbury (6 miles)
Nearest Bus Station: Aylesbury
Car Parking: Free parking for 500 cars available
Coach Parking: Free parking for 10 coaches
Souvenir Shop(s): Yes
Food & Drinks: Yes

SPECIAL INFORMATION
In addition to a large collection of locomotives and carriages, the Centre has an extensive ½ mile outdoor miniature railway system operated by the Vale of Aylesbury Model Engineering Society.

OPERATING INFORMATION
Opening Times: 2025 dates: The Museum is open and trains run on Sundays and Bank Holidays from 6th April to 20th October plus Wednesdays during the school holidays. At other times the Railway Cafe and Visitor Centre are open Monday to Friday 9.30am to 2.00pm and entrance is free.
Steam Working: All operating days.
Prices: Adult £12.50
　　　　　Child £8.50 (Under-3's travel free)
　　　　　Concessions £11.50
　　　　　Family £24.00 (1 adult + 4 children)
　　　　　Family £36.50 (2 adults + 4 children)

Detailed Directions by Car:
The Buckinghamshire Railway Centre is signposted off the A41 Aylesbury to Bicester Road at Waddesdon and off the A413 Buckingham to Aylesbury road at Whitchurch. Junctions 7, 8 and 9 of the M40 are all close by.

CALEDONIAN RAILWAY

Address: The Station, Park Road, Brechin, Angus   DD9 7AF
Telephone Nº: (01356) 622992 (Available on operating days only)
Year Formed: 1979
Location: Brechin to the Bridge of Dun
Length of Line: 4 miles

Nº of Steam Locos: 5
Nº of Other Locos: 10
Approx Nº of Visitors P.A.: 12,000
Gauge: Standard
Website: www.caledonianrailway.com
E-mail: enquiries@caledonianrailway.com

GENERAL INFORMATION

Nearest Mainline Station: Montrose (4½ miles)
Nearest Bus Station: Brechin (200 yards)
Car Parking: Ample free parking at both Stations
Coach Parking: Free parking at both Stations
Souvenir Shop(s): Yes
Food & Drinks: Light refreshments are available

SPECIAL INFORMATION

Brechin Station is the only original Terminus station in preservation.

OPERATING INFORMATION

Opening Times: 2025 dates: Although services only run on selected dates throughout the year, the Whistle Stop Cafe & Station are open most Wednesdays to Saturdays from 10.00am to 3.00pm. Please check the website for further details. Trains usually run from 11.00am to 3.00pm.
Steam Working: 19th & 20th April; 17th May; 21st & 22nd June; 13th September.
Prices: Adult Return £10.00
           Child Return £8.00   (Under-3s ride free)
           Concession Return £9.00
           Family Tickets £32.00   (2 Adult + 2 Child)
Higher fares may apply for Special Event Days.

Detailed Directions by Car:
From South: For Brechin Station, leave the A90 at the Brechin turn-off and go straight through the Town Centre. Pass the Northern Hotel, take the 2nd exit at the mini-roundabout then it is 150 yards to Park Road/St. Ninian Square; From North: For Brechin Station, leave the A90 at the Brechin turn-off and go straight through Trinity Village. Turn left at the mini-roundabout, it is then 250 yards to Park Road/St. Ninian Square. Bridge of Dun is situated half way between Brechin and Montrose. (Follow tourist signs).

CAMBRIAN HERITAGE RAILWAY

Address: Old Station Building, Oswald Road, Oswestry   SY11 4RE
Telephone Nº: (01691) 728131
Year Formed: 2009
Location of Line: Oswestry/Weston Wharf
Length of Line: 1.75 miles

Nº of Steam Locos: 4 (under repair)
Nº of Other Locos: 2 DMUs + 7 others
Approx Nº of Visitors P.A.: 15,000
Gauge: Standard
Website: www.cambrianrailways.com
E-mail: info@cambrianrailways.com

GENERAL INFORMATION

Nearest Mainline Station: Gobowen (3 miles from Oswestry – 7 miles from Llynclys)
Nearest Bus Station: Oswestry
Car Parking: Available at both sites
Coach Parking: Please contact the railway's Coach Tour officer for further information.
Souvenir Shop(s): Yes
Food & Drinks: Available

SPECIAL INFORMATION

Cambrian Heritage Railway currently operates from Oswestry station to Weston Wharf station although the eventual aim of the railway is to extend the line to Llynclys in due course.

OPERATING INFORMATION

Opening Times: 2025 dates: Open every Wednesday, Saturday, Sunday and Bank Holiday from 18th April to 7th September and also on some other dates. Santa Specials run on weekends from the end of November into December.
Please check the website for further details.
Trains run from 11.00am to 4.00pm
Steam Working: Hired steam locos operate at peak times. Please check the website for further details.
Prices: Adults £10.00
   Concessions £9.00
   Children £7.00
   Family £26.00 (2 adult + 2 child)
Note: Prices shown are for "Full Day Rover" Joint tickets. Higher fares apply on Steam-hauled days.

Detailed Directions by Car:
The Llynclys site is situated on the B4396 approximately 5 miles southwest of Oswestry, just off the A483 heading towards Welshpool. Turn left at Llyncly Crossroads towards Knockin. The entrance to the site is on the right after about 400 yards, immediately over the railway bridge. The Oswestry site is near the town centre and is clearly signposted.

CHASEWATER RAILWAY (THE COLLIERY LINE)

Address: Chasewater Country Park, Pool Lane, Burntwood WS8 7NL
Telephone Nº: (01543) 452623
Year Re-formed: 1985
Location: Chasewater Country Park, near Brownhills, Walsall
Length of Line: 2 miles

Nº of Steam Locos: 12 (4 in service)
Nº of Other Locos: 15 (3 in service)
Approx Nº of Visitors P.A.: 45,000
Gauge: Standard
Website: www.chasewaterrailway.co.uk
E-mail: admin@chasewaterrailway.co.uk

GENERAL INFORMATION

Nearest Mainline Station: Walsall or Cannock (both approximately 8 miles)
Nearest Bus Station: Lichfield (8½ miles)
Car Parking: Free parking in Chasewater Park
Coach Parking: Free parking in Chasewater Park
Souvenir Shop(s): Yes
Food & Drinks: Yes

SPECIAL INFORMATION

Chasewater Railway is based on the Cannock Chase & Wolverhampton Railway opened in 1856. The railway passed into the hands of the National Coal Board which ceased using the line in 1965. Trains operate between Brownhills West and Chasetown.

OPERATING INFORMATION

Opening Times: 2025 dates: Weekends and Bank Holidays from 18th April to September plus Sundays in October and November. Also open on some Tuesdays and/or Thursdays during the school holidays in addition to Halloween, Santa Specials and other events. Please check the website for further information. A regular service runs from 11.00am on all operating days.
Steam Working: Please check the website or phone the railway for further details.
Prices: Adult £7.95
Child £5.50 (Ages 3-15 years)
Concession £6.95
Family £23.00 (2 Adults + 2 Children)

Detailed Directions by Car:
Chasewater Country Park is situated in Brownhills off the A5 southbound near the junction of the A5 with the A452 Chester Road. Follow the Brown tourist signs on the A5 for the Country Park.

CHINNOR & PRINCES RISBOROUGH RAILWAY

Address: Station Road, Chinnor, Oxon, OX39 4ER
Telephone Nº: 07979 055366
Year Formed: 1989
Location: Chinnor to Princes Risborough
Length of Line: 4 miles

Gauge: Standard
Nº of Steam Locos: 1
Nº of Other Locos: 7
Approx Nº of Visitors P.A.: 15,000
Website: www.chinnorrailway.co.uk

GENERAL INFORMATION

Nearest Mainline Station: Princes Risborough Interchange allows direct access to Mainline trains.
Nearest Bus Station: High Wycombe (10 miles)
Car Parking: Free parking available at Chinnor
Coach Parking: Prior arrangement preferred but not necessary
Souvenir Shop(s): Yes
Food & Drinks: Soft drinks and light snacks in Station Buffet. Buffet usually available on trains.

SPECIAL INFORMATION

The Chinnor & Princes Risborough Railway operates the remaining 4 mile section of the former GWR Watlington Branch from Chinnor to Thame Junction and links with national rail services at Princes Risborough.

OPERATING INFORMATION

Opening Times: 2025 dates: Sundays and Bank Holidays from 30th March to 26th October. Please check the railway's website for details of other bookable special and evening events during the year.
Steam Working: Operates from 10.45 am to 4.35pm on most Sundays and Bank Holidays
Prices: Adult Day Rover £16.00
Resident Day Rover £11.00
Concession Day Rover £14.00
Children (Ages 3-15 years) pay £1.00
(if accompanied by a fare-paying adult)
Note: Discounts are available for advance purchases made online.

Detailed Directions by Car:
From All Parts: The railway at Chinnor is situated in Station Road just off the B4009. Junction 6 of the M40 is 4 miles away and Princes Risborough 4 miles further along the B4009. Once in Chinnor follow the brown Tourist signs to the railway.

CHOLSEY & WALLINGFORD RAILWAY

Address: Wallingford Station, 5 Hithercroft Road, Wallingford, Oxon, OX10 9GQ
Telephone Nº: (01491) 835067 (24hr info)
Year Formed: 1981
Web: www.cholsey-wallingford-railway.com
E-mail: info@cholsey-wallingford-railway.com

Location of Line: Wallingford, Oxon.
Length of Line: 2½ miles
Nº of Steam Locos: Visiting locos only
Nº of Other Locos: 5
Approx Nº of Visitors P.A.: 9,700
Gauge: Standard

GENERAL INFORMATION

Nearest Mainline Station: Joint station at Cholsey
Nearest Bus Station: Wallingford (¼ mile)
Car Parking: Off road parking available
Coach Parking: Off road parking available
Souvenir Shop(s): Yes
Food & Drinks: Yes

SPECIAL INFORMATION

The Wallingford branch (now known as "The Bunk Line") was originally intended as a through line to Princes Risborough, via Watlington, but became the first standard gauge branch of Brunel's broad-gauge London to Bristol line.

OPERATING INFORMATION

Opening Times: Selected weekends from Easter until Christmas plus Thursdays from 24th July to 14th August, with trains running from 11.00am to 4.00pm – please phone the railway or check the website for further details.
Steam Working: The railway will have visiting steam locomotives from time to time.
Please contact the railway for further information.
Prices: Adult Return £13.00
　　　　　Child Return £4.00 (Under-4s ride free)
　　　　　Compartments can be booked for £45.00
　　　　　(up to 6 Adults or 4 Adults + 4 Children)
Prices: Prices may be subject to change for Engine visits and other special events.

Detailed Directions by Car:
From All Parts: Exit from the A34 at the Milton Interchange (between E. Ilsley and Abingdon). Follow signs to Didcot and Wallingford (A4130). Take Wallingford bypass, then turn left at the first roundabout (signposted Hithercroft Road). The Station is then ½ mile on the right.

CHURNET VALLEY RAILWAY

Address: Kingsley & Froghall Station, Froghall, Stoke-on-Trent ST10 2HA
Telephone Nº: (01538) 750755
Year Formed: 1978
Location of Line: Kingsley & Froghall to Cheddleton
Length: 5¼ miles (plus a further 8 miles when operating on the Cauldon Branch)
Website: www.churnetvalleyrailway.co.uk   **E-mail:** enquiries@churnetvalleyrailway.co.uk

Nº of Steam Locos: 6 (2 in operation)
Nº of Other Locos: 11 (3 in operation)
Approx Nº of Visitors P.A.: 70,000
Gauge: Standard

GENERAL INFORMATION

Nearest Mainline Station: Stoke-on-Trent (12 miles)
Nearest Bus Station: Leek (5 miles)
Car Parking: Parking available on site
Coach Parking: Restricted space available at Kingsley & Froghall Station.
Souvenir Shop(s): Yes
Food & Drinks: Yes

SPECIAL INFORMATION

Cheddleton Station is a Grade II listed building, Consall is a sleepy halt with Victorian charm, whereas Kingsley & Froghall has been rebuilt in NSR style and includes disabled facilities and a tearoom.

OPERATING INFORMATION

Opening Times: 2025 dates: Most weekends and Wednesdays from 29th March until 19th October. Also open on Bank Holiday Mondays plus a number of other Special Event days and Polar Express Rides in November & December. Please check the website or contact the railway for further timetable details.
Steam Working: Most operating days except for Diesel Gala days.
Prices: Adult Day Rover £20.00
  Child Day Rover Free with an adult
  Concession Day Rover £16.80
Note: Fares for Special Event days are higher and advance bookings are cheaper.

Detailed Directions by Car:
From All Parts: Take the M6 to Stoke-on-Trent and follow roads to Ashbourne or Leek. Cheddleton Station is off the A520 Leek to Stone road (SatNav ST13 7EE). Kingsley & Froghall Station is off the A52 Ashbourne Road.

COLNE VALLEY RAILWAY

Address: Castle Hedingham Station, Yeldham Road, Castle Hedingham, Essex, CO9 3DZ
Telephone Nº: (01787) 461174
Year Formed: 1974
Location: 7 miles north-west of Braintree
Length of Line: Approximately 1 mile

Nº of Steam Locos: 5 (not all running)
Nº of Other Locos: 11 (includes HSTs)
Approx Nº of Visitors P.A.: 45,000
Gauge: Standard and 7¼ inches
Website: www.colnevalleyrailway.co.uk
E-mail: info@colnevalleyrailway.co.uk

GENERAL INFORMATION

Nearest Mainline Station: Braintree (7 miles)
Nearest Bus Station: Hedingham bus from Braintree stops at the Railway (except on Sundays)
Car Parking: Parking at the site
Coach Parking: Free parking at site
Souvenir Shop(s): Yes
Food & Drinks: Yes – on operational days. Also Pullman Sunday Lunches – bookings necessary.

SPECIAL INFORMATION

The railway has been re-built on a section of the old Colne Valley & Halstead Railway, with all buildings, bridges, signal boxes, etc. re-located on site.

OPERATING INFORMATION

Opening Times: 2025 dates: Steam trains run most Sundays and Bank Holiday weekends from 30th March to 26th October plus Wednesdays and some Thursdays during the School Holidays. Diesel & HST trains run some Saturdays between 3rd April and 25th October, but please check the website for details.
Steam Working: Site opens at 10.30am.
Trains run from 11.30am. Last admission 3.00pm.
Prices: Adult – Steam £15.00 Diesel £10.00
Child – Steam £9.00 Diesel £6.00
Family (2 adults + 3 children) –
Steam £43.50 Diesel £29.00
Concessions – Steam £12.00 Diesel £8.00
Note: HST prices are higher than Diesel prices

Detailed Directions by Car:
Exit the M11 at Junction 8 (Stanstead Airport) and follow the A120 eastwards to Braintree. Take the A131 northwards to High Garrett and bear left at the traffic lights onto the A1017 signposted Haverhill. Follow this road for 6 miles and the entrance to the railway is on the right past the villages of Gosfield and Sible Hedingham.

CREWE HERITAGE CENTRE

Address: Vernon Way, Crewe, CW1 2DB
Telephone Nº: (01270) 212130
Year Formed: 1987
Location of Line: Crewe Heritage Centre
Length of Line: 300 yards (Standard gauge) and 600 yards (7¼ inch gauge)

Nº of Steam Locos: Visiting locos only
Nº of Other Locos: 11 (includes HST)
Approx Nº of Visitors P.A.: 15,000
Gauge: Standard and 7¼ inches
Website: www.crewehc.org

GENERAL INFORMATION

Nearest Mainline Station: Crewe (¾ mile)
Nearest Bus Station: Crewe (½ mile)
Car Parking: Available on site (Parking is free of charge with an admission ticket)
Coach Parking: None
Souvenir Shop(s): Yes
Food & Drinks: Tea and Coffee only

SPECIAL INFORMATION

Crewe Heritage Centre is an operational base for numerous mainline steam charters with various locomotives present throughout the year.

OPERATING INFORMATION

Opening Times: Weekends and Bank Holidays from 29th March until the end of October. Open 10.00am to 4.30pm with last admissions at 3.30pm.
Steam Working: Please contact the Centre for details of steam days.
Prices: Adults £8.00
Children £6.00 (Under-5s ride free)
Concessions £6.00
Family Tickets £16.00
(2 Adults + 3 Children)

Detailed Directions by Car:
From All Parts: Exit the M6 at Junction 16 and take the A500 into Crewe. Follow the brown tourist signs for "The Railway Age". The Heritage Centre is adjacent to Crewe Railway Station and next to the Tesco Supermarket.

DARTMOUTH STEAM RAILWAY & RIVER BOAT COMPANY

Address: Queen's Park Station, Torbay Road, Paignton   TQ4 6AF
Telephone Nº: (01803) 555872
Year Formed: 1973
Location of Line: Paignton to Kingswear
Length of Line: 7 miles

Nº of Steam Locos: 4 (2 in service)
Nº of Other Locos: 6 (2 in service)
Approx Nº of Visitors P.A.: 250,000
Gauge: Standard
Website: www.dartmouthrailriver.co.uk
E-mail: carolyn@dsrrb.co.uk

GENERAL INFORMATION

Nearest Mainline Station: Paignton (adjacent)
Nearest Bus Station: Paignton (2 minutes walk)
Car Parking: Multi-storey or Mainline Station
Coach Parking: Multi-storey (3 minutes walk)
Souvenir Shop(s): Yes – at Paignton & Kingswear
Food & Drinks: Yes – at Paignton & Kingswear

SPECIAL INFORMATION

A passenger ferry is available from Kingswear Station across to Dartmouth. Combined excursions are also available including train and river trips.

OPERATING INFORMATION

Opening Times: 2025 dates: Open daily from 25th March to 2nd November and on other dates during February, March and November.
Santa Specials operate during dates in December. Please contact the railway for further information.
Steam Working: Trains run throughout the day from 10.30am to 5.00pm.
Prices: Adult Return £23.50 (Includes ferry charge)
          Child Return £16.50 (Includes ferry charge)
          Family Return £73.00
      (2 adults and 3 children – Includes ferry charge)
Note: Cheaper fares are charged for shorter journeys

Detailed Directions by Car:
From All Parts: Take the M5 to Exeter and then the A380 to Paignton.

DEAN FOREST RAILWAY

Address: Norchard Station, Forest Road; Lydney, Gloucestershire GL15 4ET
Telephone Nº: (01594) 845840
Year Formed: 1970
Location of Line: Lydney, Gloucestershire
Length of Line: 4½ miles

Nº of Steam Locos: 7 (2 in service)
Nº of Other Locos: 18 (3 in service)
Approx Nº of Visitors P.A.: 35,000
Gauge: Standard
Website: www.deanforestrailway.co.uk
E-mail: contact@deanforestrailway.co.uk

GENERAL INFORMATION

Nearest Mainline Station: Lydney (200 metres)
Nearest Bus Station: Lydney Town (400 metres)
Car Parking: 600 spaces at Norchard
Coach Parking: Ample space available
Souvenir Shop(s): Yes + a Museum
Food & Drinks: Operational days only

SPECIAL INFORMATION

Dean Forest Railway preserves the sole surviving line of the Severn and Wye Railway. The Railway has lengthened the line to a total of 4½ miles and Norchard to Parkend is now open for steam train operation giving a round trip of 9 miles.

OPERATING INFORMATION

Opening Times: 2025 dates: Norchard is open daily for viewing. Trains operate on Wednesdays, Saturdays and Sundays from 12th March to 29th October and on various other dates including Santa Specials which operate on some dates in December. Please contact the railway for further details.
Steam Working: Most services are steam-hauled – check the website or phone for details. Trains depart Norchard at various times from 10.30am to 3.38pm.
Prices: Adult Return £17.50
Child Return £9.00 (Under-3s ride free)
Note: Fares may differ for Special Events.

Detailed Directions by Car:
From M50 & Ross-on-Wye: Take the B4228 and B4234 via Coleford to reach Lydney. Norchard is located on the B4234, ¾ mile north of Lydney Town Centre; From Monmouth: Take the A4136 and B4431 onto the B4234 via Coleford; From South Wales: Take the M4 then M48 onto the A48 via Chepstow to Lydney; From Midlands/Gloucester: Take the M5 to Gloucester then the A48 to Lydney; From the West Country: Take the M4 and M48 via the 'Old' Severn Bridge to Chepstow and then the A48 to Lydney.

Derwent Valley Light Railway
(The Blackberry Line)

Address: Murton Park, Murton Lane, Murton, York   YO19 5UF
Telephone Nº: (01904) 489966
Year Formed: 1991
Location of Line: Murton, near York
Length of Line: ½ mile

Nº of Steam Locos: 1 (not in use)
Nº of Other Locos: 10
Approx Nº of Visitors P.A.: 12,000
Gauge: Standard
Website: www.dvlr.org.uk
E-mail: info@dvlr.org.uk

GENERAL INFORMATION
Nearest Mainline Station: York (4 miles)
Nearest Bus Station: York (4 miles)
Car Parking: Large free car park at the site
Coach Parking: Free at the site
Souvenir Shop(s): Yes
Food & Drinks: Available in the Museum.

SPECIAL INFORMATION
The Derwent Valley Light Railway forms part of the Yorkshire Museum of Farming at Murton Park.

OPERATING INFORMATION
Opening Times: 2025 dates: Open daily from 10.00am to 3.30pm. Santa Specials also operate on dates in December.
Steam Working: None at present
Prices: Adults £18.00   Children £15.00
            Family Tickets £48.00
            (2 adults + 3 children)
Note: Prices shown are for entry to Murton Park. Rides are free thereafter. Prices are higher on some Special Event days and for Cab rides.

Detailed Directions by Car:
From All Parts: The railway is well signposted for the Yorkshire Museum of Farming from the A64 (York to Scarborough road), the A1079 (York to Hull road) and the A166 (York to Bridlington road).

DIDCOT RAILWAY CENTRE

Address: Didcot Railway Centre, Didcot, Oxfordshire OX11 7NJ
Telephone Nº: (01235) 817200
Year Formed: 1961
Location of Line: Didcot
Length of Line: ¾ mile

Nº of Steam Locos: 28
Nº of Other Locos: 6
Gauge: Standard and 7¼ inch
Approx Nº of Visitors P.A.: 70,000
Website: www.didcotrailwaycentre.org.uk
E-mail: info@didcotrailwaycentre.org.uk

GENERAL INFORMATION

Nearest Mainline Station: Didcot Parkway adjacent
Nearest Bus Station: Buses to Didcot call at the Railway station
Car Parking: Didcot Parkway car park is adjacent and a new 1,800 space multi-storey car park in Foxhall Road is a longer walk.
Coach Parking: None
Souvenir Shop(s): Yes
Food & Drinks: Yes

SPECIAL INFORMATION

The Centre is based at a Great Western Railway engine shed and is devoted to the re-creation of part of the GWR including Brunel's broad gauge railway and a newly built replica of the Fire Fly locomotive of 1840.

OPERATING INFORMATION

Opening Times: 2025 dates: Weekends and Wednesdays from 26th February to late October (except for 12th May to 1st June) and also most days (but for Mondays & Tuesdays) during the school holidays. Weekends and Steam days open 10.30am to 5.00pm.
Steam Working: Easter Bank Holiday and every weekend from 7th June until 7th September.
Please phone or check the website for full details.
Prices: Adult £14.00 to £20.50
Child £8.50 to £13.00
Concessions £10.00 to £19.00
Family tickets £38.00 to £65.00
(2 adults + 2 children)
Note: The prices shown above are 'Gift Aid' rates.

Detailed Directions by Car:
From East & West: Take the M4 to Junction 13 then the A34 and A4130 (follow brown Tourist signs to Didcot Railway Centre); From North: The Centre is signed from the A34 to A4130.

Doon Valley Railway

Address: Dunaskin Bridge, Dalmellington Road, Waterside, Patna, Ayrshire KA6 7JH
Telephone Nº: (01292) 313579 (Evenings & Weekends)
Year Formed: 1974
Location of Line: Dunaskin Ironworks
Length of Line: One third of a mile

Nº of Steam Locos: 7
Nº of Other Locos: 10
Approx Nº of Visitors P.A.: 3,500
Gauge: Standard
Website: www.doonvalleyrailway.co.uk
E-mail: info@doonvalleyrailway.co.uk

GENERAL INFORMATION

Nearest Mainline Station: Ayr (10 miles)
Nearest Bus Station: A half-hourly bus service operates from Ayr. Please phone (01292) 613500 for more information.
Car Parking: Free parking available at the site
Coach Parking: Free parking available at the site
Souvenir Shop(s): Yes
Food & Drinks: Cafe available on site

SPECIAL INFORMATION

Formerly known as The Scottish Industrial Railway Centre the Railway is operated by the Ayrshire Railway Preservation Group.

OPERATING INFORMATION

Opening Times: 2025 operating dates: 4th & 25th May then every Sunday until 28th September. Trains run from 11.00am until 4.00pm
Steam Working: On all operating dates.
Prices: Adult Return £8.00
Child Return £4.00 (Under-3s ride free)

Detailed Directions by Car:
From All Parts: Dunaskin is situated adjacent to the A713 Ayr to Castle Douglas road, approximately 10 miles to the southwest of Ayr.

EAST ANGLIAN RAILWAY MUSEUM

Address: Chappel & Wakes Colne Station, Colchester, Essex   CO6 2DS
Telephone Nº: (01206) 242524
Year Formed: 1969
Location of Line: 6 miles west of Colchester on Marks Tey to Sudbury branch
Length of Line: A third of a mile

Nº of Steam Locos: 3
Nº of Other Locos: 2
Approx Nº of Visitors P.A.: 40,000
Gauge: Standard
Website: www.earm.co.uk
E-mail: information@earm.co.uk

GENERAL INFORMATION

Nearest Mainline Station: Chappel & Wakes Colne (adajcent)
Nearest Bus Stop: Wakes Colne Post Office (400 yards)
Car Parking: Free parking at site
Coach Parking: Free parking at site
Souvenir Shop(s): Yes
Food & Drinks: Snacks and drinks are available

SPECIAL INFORMATION

The museum has the most comprehensive collection of railway architecture & engineering in the region. The railway also has a miniature railway that usually operates on steam days.

OPERATING INFORMATION

Opening Times: 2025 dates: Open from 10.00am to 5.00pm (until 4.00pm from November to March) on Weekends and also on Wednesdays for Museum viewing.
Steam Working: Steam days are held most months from March to August but please check the website for full details. Bank Holidays are also Steam days. Please check the website for further details.
Prices: Adult £8.00 (static viewing) £11.50 Steam
           Child £4.00 (static viewing) £8.50 Steam
Children under the age of 4 are admitted free of charge.

Detailed Directions by Car:
From North & South: Turn off the A12 south west of Colchester onto the A1124 (formerly the A604). The Museum is situated just off the A1124; From West: Turn off the A120 just before Marks Tey (signposted).

32

East Kent Railway

Address: Station Road, Shepherdswell, Dover, Kent   CT15 7PD
Telephone Nº: (01304) 832042
Year Formed: 1985
Location of Line: Between Shepherdswell and Eythorne
Length of Line: 2 miles

Nº of Steam Locos: 2 (1 not in use)
Nº of Other Locos: 4 + DEMUs
Approx Nº of Visitors P.A.: 15,500
Gauge: Standard gauge and also 5 inch and 7¼ inch miniature gauges
Website: www.eastkentrailway.co.uk

GENERAL INFORMATION

Nearest Mainline Station: Shepherdswell (50 yards)
Car Parking: Available Shepherdswell and Eythorne
Coach Parking: Available at both stations by prior arrangement.
Souvenir Shop(s): Yes
Food & Drinks: Yes – both hot and cold available

SPECIAL INFORMATION

The East Kent Railway was originally built between 1911 and 1917 to service Tilmanstone Colliery. Closed in the mid-1980's, the railway was re-opened in 1995.

OPERATING INFORMATION

Opening Times: The 2025 operating season runs from 30th March until 19th October. Trains operate every Sunday and Bank Holiday during this period plus the last Saturday in July and all Saturdays in August. Also during some other special events including Halloween and Santa Specials.
Steam Working: Please check website for details
Prices: Adult   £10.00
   Child   £6.00 (Under-2s free)
   Concession   £6.00
   Family   £30.00 (2 Adults and 2 Children)

Detailed Directions by Car:
From the A2: Take the turning to Shepherdswell and continue to the village. Pass the shop on the left and cross the railway bridge. Take the next left (Station Road) signposted at the traffic lights for the EKR; From the A256: Take the turning for Eythorne at the roundabout on the section between Eastry and Whitfield. Follow the road through Eythorne. Further on you will cross the railway line and enter Shepherdswell. After a few hundred yards take the right turn signposted for the EKR.

East Lancashire Railway

Address: Bolton Street Station, Bury, Lancashire BL9 0EY
Telephone Nº: (0333) 320-2830
Year Formed: 1968
Location of Line: Heywood, Bury, Ramsbottom and Rawtenstall
Length of Line: 12 miles

Nº of Steam Locos: 13
Nº of Other Locos: 37
Approx Nº of Visitors P.A.: 205,000
Gauge: Standard
Website: www.eastlancsrailway.org.uk
E-mail: enquiries@eastlancsrailway.org.uk

GENERAL INFORMATION

Nearest Mainline Station: Manchester (then Metrolink to Bury)
Nearest Bus Station: ¼ mile
Car Parking: Adjacent
Coach Parking: Adjacent
Souvenir Shop(s): Yes
Food & Drinks: Yes

SPECIAL INFORMATION

Originally opened in 1846, the East Lancashire Railway was re-opened in 1987 and is also the location of the Bury Transport Museum

OPERATING INFORMATION

Opening Times: Every weekend & Bank Holiday 9.00am to 5.00pm. Also Wednesdays to Fridays during school holidays. A number of special events (including Santa Specials) run during the year. Please check the website for details.
Steam Working: Most trains are steam-hauled. Saturdays alternate Steam & Diesel. Engines are in steam on most Sundays.
Prices: Adult Return £20.00
Child Return £13.00 (Ages 3 to 15 years)
Young Person Return £16.00 (Ages 16 & 17)
Family Return £34.50 (1 Adult + 2 Child)
Family Return £47.00 (2 Adult + 3 Child)
Above prices are for advance purchases of Day Rover Tickets but those bought on the day cost more. Cheaper fares are available for shorter journeys.

Detailed Directions by Car:
From All Parts: Exit the M66 at Junction 2 and take the A56 into Bury. Follow the brown tourist signs and turn right into Bolton Street at the junction with the A58. The station is about 150 yards on the right.

East Somerset Railway

Address: Cranmore Railway Station, Shepton Mallet, Somerset BA4 4QP
Telephone Nº: (01749) 880417
Year Formed: 1971
Location of Line: Cranmore, off A361 between Frome and Shepton Mallet
Length of Line: 3 miles

Nº of Steam Locos: 3
Nº of Other Locos: 5
Approx Nº of Visitors P.A.: 25,000
Gauge: Standard
Website: www.eastsomersetrailway.com
E-mail: info@eastsomersetrailway.com

GENERAL INFORMATION

Nearest Mainline Station: Castle Cary (10 miles)
Nearest Bus Station: Shepton Mallet (3 miles)
Car Parking: Space for 100 cars available
Coach Parking: Yes
Souvenir Shop(s): Yes
Food & Drinks: Whistlestop Café is open on operating days.

SPECIAL INFORMATION

Footplate experience courses, Sunday lunches, Cream and Sparkling Afternoon Teas are all available for pre-booking as are a number of other family events held throughout the year – phone (01749) 880417 for further details.

OPERATING INFORMATION

Opening Times: The office and shop are open Tuesday to Friday from 10.00am to 3.30pm when trains are not running (4.30pm on operating days).
Steam Working: 2025 dates: Weekends and Bank Holidays from 8th March to 26th October, Wednesdays from 7th May to 29th October and most Thursdays from 5th June to 25th September. Santa Specials run on some December weekends. Special events on some other dates.
Trains run from 11.00am to 3.30pm.
Prices: Adult Day Rover £15.00
  Child Day Rover £10.00
  Concession Day Rover £12.00
  Family Tickets £32.00 and £42.00
Note: Prices are more expensive on Special event days and season tickets are also available.

Detailed Directions by Car:
From the North: Take A367/A37 to Shepton Mallet then turn left onto A361 to Frome. Carry on to Shepton Mallet and 9 miles after Frome turn left at Cranmore; From the South: Take A36 to Frome bypass then A361 to Cranmore; From the West: Take A371 from Wells to Shepton Mallet, then A361 to Frome (then as above).

ECCLESBOURNE VALLEY RAILWAY

Address: Station Road, Coldwell Street, Wirksworth   DE4 4FB
Telephone Nº: (01629) 823076
Year Formed: 2000
Location of Line: Ravenstor to Duffield
Length of Line: 8½ miles

Nº of Steam Locos: 4 (2 operational)
Nº of Other Locos: 12 (including DMUs)
Approx Nº of Visitors P.A.: 25,000
Gauge: Standard
Website: www.e-v-r.com
Email: info@e-v-r.com

GENERAL INFORMATION

Nearest Mainline Station: Duffield (adjacent)
Nearest Bus Station: Derby (13 miles)
Car Parking: Available at the Station
Coach Parking: Available at Wirksworth Station
Souvenir Shop(s): Yes
Food & Drinks: Yes

SPECIAL INFORMATION

The line was restored section by section and the Railway opened all 8½ miles in April 2011.

OPERATING INFORMATION

Opening Times: 2025 dates: Weekends, Bank Holidays and school holidays from 22nd February until 9th November. Also open on various other days from May to September. Timetables vary depending on the date. Please check the website for further details.
Steam Working: Most Weekends and Bank Holidays from 9th April to 9th November except for special Diesel Events.
Prices: Adult Day Rover £21.50
              Child Day Rover £11.00 (Under-5s free)
              Concessions Day Rover £19.00
              Family Day Rover £43.00
Note: Prices vary depending on journey length and discounts are available for advance bookings.

Detailed Directions by Car:
From All Parts: Exit the M1 at Junction 26 and take the A610 Ambergate then the A6 to Whatstandwell. Turn left onto the B5035 to Wirksworth and the station is at the bottom of the hill as you enter the town.

EDEN VALLEY RAILWAY

Address: Warcop Station, Warcop, Appleby, Cumbria CA16 6PR
Telephone Nº: (01768) 342309
Year Formed: 1995
Location: Warcop Station to Southfields
Length: Approximately 2¼ miles

Nº of Steam Locos: None
Nº of Other Locos: 9
Approx Nº of Visitors P.A.: Not known
Gauge: Standard
Website: www.evr-cumbria.org.uk
E-mail: enquiries@evr-cumbria.org.uk

GENERAL INFORMATION

Nearest Mainline Station: Appleby (5½ miles)
Car Parking: Warcop Station only
Coach Parking: Warcop Station only
Souvenir Shop(s): Yes – in the 'Buffer Stop' carriage
Food & Drinks: In the 'Buffer Stop' carriage.

SPECIAL INFORMATION

The Eden Valley Railway Trust is working towards the restoration of the Warcop to Appleby-in-Westmorland Line.

OPERATING INFORMATION

Opening Times: 2025 dates: Sundays from 30th March to 27th October plus Tuesdays & Wednesdays from 16th July to 21st August. Open from 10.30am to 5.00pm
Steam Working: None at present
Prices: Adults £10.00
Children £4.00 (Under-5s free)
Family £22.00 (2 Adults + all Children)
Note: Children under the age of 15 must be accompanied by an adult. Also, 'Driver for a Fiver' Trips are available.

Detailed Directions by Car:
From the West: Exit the M6 at Junction 40 and head east on the A66 for approximately 18 miles. Turn right at the Warcop road junction, signposted for Warcop and the Warcop Training Centre. Turn left immediately before the railway bridge and follow this road to the visitor entrance; From the East: Take the A66 over Stainmore and past Brough before turning left at the Warcop road junction signposted for Warcop and the Warcop Training Centre. Then as above.

EMBSAY & BOLTON ABBEY STEAM RAILWAY

Address: Bolton Abbey Station, Bolton Abbey, Skipton BD23 6AF
Telephone Nº: (01756) 710614
Year Formed: 1968
Gauge: Standard
Website: www.embsayboltonabbeyrailway.org.uk

Location of Line: 2 miles east of Skipton
Length of Line: 4½ miles
Nº of Steam Locos: 15 (not all running)
Nº of Other Locos: 12 (not all running)
Approx Nº of Visitors P.A.: 110,000

GENERAL INFORMATION

Nearest Mainline Station: Skipton (2 miles) and Ilkley (3 miles)
Nearest Bus Station: Skipton (2 miles), Ilkley (3 mls)
Car Parking: Large car park at both Stations
Coach Parking: Large coach park at both Stations
Souvenir Shop(s): Yes
Food & Drinks: Yes – Cafe + Buffet cars

SPECIAL INFORMATION

The line extension to Bolton Abbey opened in 1998.

OPERATING INFORMATION

Opening Times: 2025 dates: Weekends from 1st February to 26th October, most Tuesdays and Wednesdays from 4th March to 28th October and Thursdays in August and September.
Santa Specials run on weekends in December. Please check the website for full details.
Steam Working: Steam trains depart Embsay Station at 10.30am, 12.00pm, 1.30pm, 3.00pm and 4.30pm on most days during the Main Season. Contact the railway for further details.
Prices: Adult Return £15.00
Child Return £8.50
Concession Return £14.00
Family Ticket £39.00 (2 adult + 2 children)
Different fares may apply on special event days.

Detailed Directions by Car:
From All Parts: Embsay Station is off the A59 Skipton bypass by the Harrogate Road. Bolton Abbey Station is off the A59 at Bolton Abbey.

Epping Ongar Railway

Address: Ongar Station, Ongar, Essex, CM5 9BN
Telephone Nº: (01277) 365200
Year Formed: 2004
Location of Line: Epping Forest to Ongar
Length of Line: 6.3 miles

Nº of Steam Locos: 5
Nº of Other Locos: 11
Approx Nº of Visitors P.A.: 40,000
Gauge: Standard gauge
Website: www.eorailway.co.uk
E-mail: enquiries@eorailway.co.uk

GENERAL INFORMATION

Nearest Mainline Station: Epping Underground – Central line (7½ miles to Ongar Station)
Nearest Bus Station: Epping (7½ miles)
Car Parking: Limited parking close to Ongar Station and plenty of spaces at Epping Station. No parking is available at North Weald Station.
Coach Parking: By arrangement only
Souvenir Shop(s): Yes
Food & Drinks: Available at Ongar and North Weald

SPECIAL INFORMATION

A frequent heritage bus service (number 339) runs from Epping Tube Station (and Shenfield Train Station during the summer) to the railway every operating day. A further bus service (number 381) runs from Epping to North Weald on selected dates.

OPERATING INFORMATION

Opening Times: 2025 dates: Weekends and Bank Holidays from 5th April to 28th September and for Santa Specials during December. Also open on most Wednesdays during the school holidays.
Steam Working: Most operating days.
Prices: Adults £19.50
Children £1.00 (with a paying adult)
Concessions £18.50
Note: Under-3s ride free of charge.

Detailed Directions by Car:
For North Weald Station: Exit the M11 at Junction 7 and follow the A414 towards Chelmsford and North Weald. Take the 3rd exit at the 2nd roundabout ('The Talbot' pub on the left) and follow the road into North Weald village. Station Road is on the left just after leaving the village. For Ongar Station: Exit the M11 at Junction 7 and follow the A414 towards Chelmsford and North Weald. Follow the road for approximately 5 miles going straight on at two roundabouts. At the 3rd roundabout (BP garage on the left) take the third exit towards Ongar. Epping Ongar Railway is located on the right hand side after approximately 400 yards.

Foxfield Steam Railway

Address: Caverswall Road Station, Blythe Bridge, Stoke-on-Trent, Staffs. ST11 9BG
Telephone Nº: (01782) 396210
Year Formed: 1967
Location of Line: Blythe Bridge
Length of Line: 3½ miles

Nº of Steam Locos: 20 (6 in service)
Nº of Other Locos: 12
Gauge: Standard
Approx Nº of Visitors P.A.: Over 25,000
Website: www.foxfieldrailway.co.uk
E-mail: flrsenquiries@foxfieldrailway.co.uk

GENERAL INFORMATION

Nearest Mainline Station: Blythe Bridge (¼ mile)
Nearest Bus Station: Hanley (5 miles)
Car Parking: Space for 300 cars available
Coach Parking: Space for 6 coaches available
Souvenir Shop(s): Yes
Food & Drinks: Yes – Buffet and Real Ale Bar

SPECIAL INFORMATION

The Railway is a former Colliery railway built in 1893 to take coal from Foxfield Colliery. It has the steepest Standard Gauge adhesion worked gradient in the UK and a Museum housing some unique exhibits.

OPERATING INFORMATION

Opening Times: 2025 dates: Usually Sundays and Bank Holidays from 30th March to 12th October. Please check the website for further details.
Steam Working: Most Knotty Heritage Days and during other Special Events.
Prices: Adult Day Rover £15.00
Child Day Rover £8.00 (ages 3 to 16 years)
Concession Day Rover £12.00
Note: Fares for Special Events may vary and upgrades to 1st class cost £15.00.

Detailed Directions by Car:
From South: Exit M6 at Junction 14 onto the A34 to Stone then the A520 to Meir and the A50 to Blythe Bridge; From North: Exit M6 at Junction 15 then the A500 to Stoke-on-Trent and the A50 to Blythe Bridge; From East: Take the A50 to Blythe Bridge. Once in Blythe Bridge, turn by the Mainline crossing.

GLOUCESTERSHIRE WARWICKSHIRE RAILWAY

Address: The Station, Toddington, Cheltenham, Gloucestershire GL54 5DT
Telephone Nº: (01242) 621405
Year Formed: 1981
Location of Line: Broadway, near the A46 to Cheltenham Racecourse
Length of Line: 14 miles

Nº of Steam Locos: 8
Nº of Other Locos: 14
Approx Nº of Visitors P.A.: 100,000
Gauge: Standard and Narrow gauge
Website: www.gwsr.com
E-mail: info@gwsr.com

GENERAL INFORMATION

Nearest Mainline Station: Cheltenham Spa, Ashchurch or Evesham
Nearest Bus Station: Cheltenham
Car Parking: Parking available at Toddington and Cheltenham Racecourse Stations
Coach Parking: As above, by prior arrangement
Souvenir Shop(s): Yes
Food & Drinks: Available

SPECIAL INFORMATION

The railway now extends 14 miles from Broadway to Cheltenham Racecourse but the Locomotive Departments are housed at Toddington where the Railway first started.

OPERATING INFORMATION

Opening Times: 2025 dates: Weekends and Bank Holidays from 1st March to 2nd November, also most Tuesdays and Wednesdays from 1st April to 29th October and Thursdays from 29th May to 30th October. Santa Specials run at weekends in November and December as do other Holiday Services in January.
Steam Working: Every operating day, though not every service is steam-hauled on most days.
Prices: Adult Day Rover £28.00
 Child Day Rover £13.00
 Family Day Rover £75.00 (2 adult + 3 child)
 Extended Family (with 4 adults) £130.00
Note: Under 5's travel free of charge except on some Special Event days & advance tickets are cheaper.

Detailed Directions by Car:
Toddington is 11 miles north east of Cheltenham, 5 miles south of Broadway just off the B4632 (old A46). Exit the M5 at Junction 9 towards Stow-on-the-Wold for the B4632. The Railway is clearly visible from the B4632.

GREAT CENTRAL RAILWAY

Address: Great Central Station, Great Central Road, Loughborough, Leicestershire   LE11 1RW
Telephone Nº: (01509) 632323
Year Formed: 1969
Location: Loughborough to Leicester
Length of Line: 8 miles

Nº of Steam Locos: 16 (9 in service)
Nº of Other Locos: 13 + 2 DMUs
Approx Nº of Visitors P.A.: 125,000
Gauge: Standard
Website: www.gcrailway.co.uk
E-mail: sales@gcrailway.co.uk

GENERAL INFORMATION

Nearest Mainline Station: Loughborough (1 mile)
Nearest Bus Station: Loughborough (½ mile)
Car Parking: Street parking outside the Station
Coach Parking: Car parks at Quorn & Woodhouse, Rothley and Leicester North
Souvenir Shop(s): Yes
Food & Drinks: Yes – Buffet or Restaurant cars are usually available for snacks or other meals

SPECIAL INFORMATION

The Railway is working towards linking up with the currently separate Great Central Railway (Nottingham) at Loughborough Junction. In addition services on the Mountsorrel Branch Line are now running and full details appear on the website.

OPERATING INFORMATION

Opening Times: 2025 dates: Weekends from 1st February to 15th November. Santa Trains then operate until the end of the year.
Please check the railway website for further details.
Steam Working: Weekends, Bank Holidays and some Special Events throughout the year.
Prices: Adult Day Ticket £26.00
   Child Day Ticket £14.00
   Family Day Ticket £57.00
               (2 adults + 3 children)
   Family Day Ticket £42.00
               (1 adult + 3 children)
Note: Lower prices available for shorter journeys.

Detailed Directions by Car:
Great Central Road is on the South East side of Loughborough and is clearly signposted from the A6 Leicester Road and A60 Nottingham Road.

GREAT CENTRAL RAILWAY (NOTTINGHAM)

Address: Nottingham Transport Heritage Centre, Mere Way, Ruddington, Nottingham NG11 6NX
Telephone Nº: (0115) 940-5705
Fax Nº: (0115) 940-5905
Year Formed: 1990 (Opened in 1994)
Location of Line: Ruddington to Loughborough Junction

Length of Line: 9 miles
Nº of Steam Locos: 9
Nº of Other Locos: 12
Approx Nº of Visitors P.A.: 15,000
Gauge: Standard
Website: www.gcrn.co.uk

GENERAL INFORMATION
Nearest Mainline Station: Nottingham (5 miles)
Nearest Bus Station: Nottingham
Car Parking: Available on site
Coach Parking: Free parking at site
Souvenir Shop(s): Yes
Food & Drinks: Yes

SPECIAL INFORMATION
The Railway is working towards linking up with the currently separate Great Central Railway at Loughborough Junction.

OPERATING INFORMATION
Opening Times: 2025 dates: Selected weekends and Bank Holidays from 5th April until September. Please check the website for updated information. Open 10.45am to 5.00pm.
Steam Working: Please check website for details
Prices: Adult £15.00
Child £1.00 (Ages 3 to 15 with an adult)
Family £25.00 (2 adults + 3 children)
Note: Prices shown above are for unlimited day rover tickets.

Detailed Directions by Car:
From All Parts: The centre is situated off the A60 Nottingham to Loughborough Road and is signposted just south of the traffic lights at Ruddington.

Gwili Railway

Address: Abergwili Junction Station, Abergwili, Carmarthen SA31 2DG
Telephone Nº: (01267) 238213
E-mail: info@gwili-railway.co.uk
Year Formed: 1975
Location of Line: Nr Carmarthen, S. Wales
Length of Line: 5 miles

Nº of Steam Locos: 6
Nº of Other Locos: 3
Approx Nº of Visitors P.A.: 20,000
Gauge: Standard
Website: www.gwili-railway.co.uk
E-mail: info@gwili-railway.co.uk

GENERAL INFORMATION

Nearest Mainline Station: Carmarthen (3 miles)
Nearest Bus Station: Carmarthen (3 miles)
Car Parking: Free parking at Bronwydd Arms
Coach Parking: Free parking at Bronwydd Arms
Souvenir Shop(s): Yes
Food & Drinks: Yes

SPECIAL INFORMATION

Gwili Railway was the first Standard Gauge preserved railway in West Wales. There is a riverside picnic area and Miniature railway at Llwyfan Cerrig Station and there is a Signal Box Museum at Bronwydd Arms. A new extension to Abergwili Junction is now operational.

OPERATING INFORMATION

Opening Times: 2025 dates: Open most Sundays, Wednesdays, Thursdays & Bank Holidays from 2nd April to 28th September and also on Tuesdays from 22nd July to 19th August. Please contact the railway for information about Special Events.
Steam Working: All advertised trains are steam hauled. Trains run from 11.00am to 3.00pm.
Prices: A range of Vintage Train Rides and Experiences operate with prices starting at £17.00 for Adults. Please check the railway's website for full details.

Detailed Directions by Car:
Take the M4 & A48 to Carmarthen and join the A40 at the Pensarn roundabout (3rd exit) then continue to the second roundabout signed A485/Steam Railway. Turn left and car park is about 100 yards on left.

Helston Railway

Address: Trevarno Farm, Prospidnick, Helston, Cornwall   TR13 0RY
Contact Telephone N°: (01326) 572977
Year Formed: 2002
Location: Trevarno Farm, Helston to Truthal Halt
Length of Line: 1 mile

N° of Steam Locos: 2
N° of Other Locos: 2 (plus 1 DMU)
Approx N° of Visitors P.A.: 5,000
Gauge: Standard
Website: www.helstonrailway.co.uk
E-mail: info@helstonrailway.co.uk

GENERAL INFORMATION

Nearest Mainline Station: Camborne (6 miles)
Nearest Bus Station: Camborne
Car Parking: Free parking at Prospidnick Halt
Coach Parking: At Trevano Farm
Souvenir Shop(s): Yes
Food & Drinks: Buffet & Restaurant cars are open.

SPECIAL INFORMATION

The Helston Railway was formed in 2002 and has reinstated a 1 mile section of track which is open for rides. The long term aim is to reopen a 3 mile section of the line to reach the outskirts of Helston Water-ma-Trout.

OPERATING INFORMATION

Opening Times: Every Thursday, Sunday and Bank Holiday Monday from Easter until 30th October plus additional dates during the school holidays and Santa Specials on December weekends.
Please check the website for timetable information. Trains run hourly from 10.30am to 3.30pm.
Steam Working: Selected days during the season. Please contact the railway for details.
Prices: Adults £9.50
    Children £6.50
    Under-5s ride free of charge
    Family Ticket £28.00 (2 adults + 3 children)
Note: Access to the railway is via Trevarno Farm car park where free parking is available.

Detailed Directions by Car:
The railway is situated 1½ miles to the north of Helston, just off the B3303 between Crowntown and Nancegollan.

Isle of Wight Steam Railway

Address: The Railway Station, Havenstreet, Near Ryde, Isle of Wight PO33 4DS
Telephone Nº: (01983) 882204
Year Formed: 1971 (re-opened)
Location: Smallbrook Junction to Wootton
Length of Line: 5 miles

Nº of Steam Locos: 12
Nº of Other Locos: 3
Approx Nº of Visitors P.A.: 110,000
Gauge: Standard
Website: www.iwsteamrailway.co.uk
E-mail: info@iwsteamrailway.co.uk

GENERAL INFORMATION

Nearest Mainline Station: Smallbrook Junction (direct interchange)
Nearest Bus: From Ryde & Newport direct
Car Parking: Free parking at Havenstreet & Wootton Stations
Coach Parking: Free at Havenstreet Station
Souvenir Shop(s): Yes – at Havenstreet Station
Food & Drinks: Yes – at Havenstreet Station

SPECIAL INFORMATION

The IWSR uses mostly Victorian & Edwardian locomotives and carriages to recreate the atmosphere of an Isle of Wight branch line railway.

OPERATING INFORMATION

Opening Times: 2025 dates: Most days in April & May and daily (except some Fridays & Mondays) from the 24th May to 2nd November.
Santa Specials operated on weekends and some other dates in December.
Please check the website for further information.
Steam Working: 10.05am to 4.20pm (depending on the Station and also the time of year)
Prices: Adult Day Ticket £25.00 to £35.00
Child Day Ticket £12.50 to £17.50
(Under-5s travel free)
Family Day Ticket £50.00 to £70.00
(2 adults + 4 children)

Detailed Directions by Car:
To reach the Isle of Wight head for the Ferry ports at Lymington, Southampton or Portsmouth. From all parts of the Isle of Wight, head for Havenstreet (which is located 3 miles from Ryde and 3 miles from Newport), and follow the brown tourist signs.

KEIGHLEY & WORTH VALLEY RAILWAY

Address: The Station, Haworth, Keighley, West Yorkshire BD22 8NJ
Telephone Nº: (01535) 645214 (enquiries)
Year Formed: 1962 (Line re-opened 1968)
Location of Line: From Keighley southwards through Haworth to Oxenhope
Length of Line: 5 miles

Nº of Steam Locos: 21
Nº of Other Locos: 9 (plus DMUs)
Approx Nº of Visitors P.A.: 120,000
Gauge: Standard
Website: www.kwvr.co.uk
E-mail: admin@kwvr.co.uk

GENERAL INFORMATION

Nearest Mainline Station: Keighley (adjacent)
Nearest Bus Station: Keighley (5 minutes walk)
Car Parking: Parking at Keighley, Ingrow, Haworth (charged) and Oxenhope
Coach Parking: At Ingrow & Oxenhope (phone in advance)
Souvenir Shop(s): Yes – at Keighley, Oxenhope & Haworth (whose shop also sells books/DVDs)
Food & Drinks: Yes – at Keighley & Oxenhope when trains run.

SPECIAL INFORMATION

At Ingrow Station, there are two railway museums. Please see www.railstory.co.uk for information.

OPERATING INFORMATION

Opening Times: 2025 dates: Weekends, Bank Holidays and School Holidays throughout the year. Daily from 16th July to 31st August, plus some other mid-week days in May and June and Santa Specials during December.
Steam Working: Steam runs from mid-morning on all operating days including when Santa Specials operate (pre-booking required for Santa Specials).
Prices: Adult Day Rover £22.00
 Child Day Rover £11.00
 Family Day Rovers £27.50 to £55.00

Detailed Directions by Car:
Exit the M62 at Junction 26 and take the M606 to its' end. Follow the ring-road signs around Bradford to Shipley. Take the A650 through Bingley to Keighley and follow the brown tourist signs to the railway. Alternatively, take the A6033 from Hebden Bridge to Oxenhope and follow the brown signs to Oxenhope or Haworth Stations.

THE KEITH & DUFFTOWN RAILWAY

Address: Dufftown Station, Dufftown, Banffshire, AB55 4BB
Telephone Nº: (01340) 821181
Year Formed: 2000
Location of Line: Keith to Dufftown
Length of Line: 11 miles

Nº of Steam Locos: None at present
Nº of Other Locos: 6 DMU + 3 shunters
Approx Nº of Visitors P.A.: Not known
Gauge: Standard
Web: www.keith-dufftown-railway.co.uk

GENERAL INFORMATION

Nearest Mainline Station: Keith (½ mile)
Nearest Bus Station: Elgin (Bus routes travel to both Keith and Dufftown)
Car Parking: Available at both Stations
Coach Parking: Available at both Stations
Souvenir Shop(s): Yes – at Keith Town Station
Food & Drinks: Available at Dufftown Station

SPECIAL INFORMATION

The Keith and Dufftown Railway is an eleven mile line linking the World's Malt Whisky Capital, Dufftown, to the market town of Keith. The line, which was reopened by volunteers during 2000 and 2001, passes through some of Scotland's most picturesque scenery, with forest and farmland, lochs and glens, castles and distilleries.

OPERATING INFORMATION

Opening Times: 2025 dates: Most Fridays and Weekends from 5th April until 21st September and also on Weekends in December. Trains depart Dufftown from 10.30am until 3.30pm.
Steam Working: None at present
Prices: Adult Single £8.00
Child Single £4.00 (under-5s free)
Concessionary Single £7.00
Family Single £18.00
Note: 1st class & Specials are more expensive but shorter journeys are cheaper.

Detailed Directions by Car:
Keith Town Station is located in Keith, on the A96 Aberdeen to Inverness Road; Dufftown Station is about 1 mile to the north of the Dufftown Town Centre just off the A941 road to Elgin.

Kent & East Sussex Railway

Address: Tenterden Town Station, Tenterden, Kent   TN30 6HE
Telephone Nº: (01580) 765155
Year Formed: 1974
Location of Line: Tenterden, Kent to Bodiam, East Sussex
Length of Line: 10½ miles

Nº of Steam Locos: 16
Nº of Other Locos: 6
Approx Nº of Visitors P.A.: 99,000
Gauge: Standard
Website: www.kesr.org.uk
E-mail: enquiries@kesr.org.uk

GENERAL INFORMATION

Nearest Mainline Station: Headcorn (8 miles)
Nearest Bus Station: Tenterden
Car Parking: Free parking available at Tenterden Town and Northiam Stations
Coach Parking: Tenterden & Northiam
Souvenir Shop(s): Yes
Food & Drinks: Yes

SPECIAL INFORMATION

Built as Britain's first light railway, the K&ESR opened in 1900 and was epitomised by sharp curved and steep gradients and to this day retains a charm and atmosphere all of its own.

OPERATING INFORMATION

Opening Times: 2025 dates: Weekends, Wednesdays, Bank Holidays, and School holidays from 1st February to 28th September, most days in July and August plus Weekends in October and December. Please check the website for daily running times and events.
Trains depart from 10.20am.
Steam Working: Every operational day
Prices: Adult Ticket – £32.50
Child Ticket – £15.00
Concession Ticket – £29.00
Family Tickets – £75.00 to £85.00
Note: Prices shown are for All Day travel tickets and pre-booked tickets are cheaper.

Detailed Directions by Car:
From London and Kent Coast: Travel to Ashford (M20) then take the A28 to Tenterden; From Sussex Coast: Take the A28 from Hastings to Northiam.

LAKESIDE & HAVERTHWAITE RAILWAY

Address: Haverthwaite Station, near Ulverston, Cumbria LA12 8AL
Telephone Nº: (015395) 31594
Year Formed: 1973
Location: Haverthwaite to Lakeside
Length of Line: 3½ miles

Nº of Steam Locos: 7
Nº of Other Locos: 6
Approx Nº of Visitors P.A.: 190,000
Gauge: Standard
Website: www.lakesiderailway.co.uk
E-mail: info@lakesiderailway.co.uk

GENERAL INFORMATION

Nearest Mainline Station: Ulverston (7 miles)
Nearest Bus Station: Haverthwaite (100 yards)
Car Parking: Approximately 150 spaces available – £2.00 charge for all day parking.
Coach Parking: Free parking at site
Souvenir Shop(s): Yes
Food & Drinks: Yes

SPECIAL INFORMATION

Tickets which include train ride followed by a cruise on Lake Windermere or a visit to the Aquarium of the Lakes are also available from the Railway.

OPERATING INFORMATION

Opening Times: 2025 dates: Daily from 5th April to 2nd November inclusive. Also open for Santa Specials during weekends in December.
A number of other Special Events run throughout the year. Please check the website for further details.
Steam Working: Daily unless otherwise advertised
Prices: Adult Return £12.00 (Day Rover £35.00)
Child Return £7.00 (Day Rover £20.00)
(Under-3's ride for free)
Family Ticket £35.00 (2 adult + 3 child)
Note: Prices vary for Special Events and individual fares are available for combined tickets including access to other attractions.

Detailed Directions by Car:
From All Parts: Exit the M6 at Junction 36 and follow the brown tourist signs.

THE LAVENDER LINE

Address: Isfield Station, Isfield, near Uckfield, East Sussex TN22 5XB
Telephone N°: (01825) 750515
Year Formed: 1992
Location of Line: East Sussex between Lewes and Uckfield
Length of Line: 1 mile

N° of Steam Locos: 3 (1 in service)
N° of Other Locos: 4 + 2 DEMUs
Approx N° of Visitors P.A.: 12,500
Gauge: Standard
Website: www.lavender-line.co.uk
E-mail: enquiries@lavender-line.co.uk

GENERAL INFORMATION

Nearest Mainline Station: Uckfield (3 miles)
Nearest Bus Station: Uckfield (3 miles)
Car Parking: Free parking on site
Coach Parking: Can cater for coach parties – please contact the Railway.
Souvenir Shop: Yes
Food & Drinks: Yes – Cinders Buffet

SPECIAL INFORMATION

Isfield Station has been restored as a Southern Railway country station complete with the original London Brighton & South Coast Railway signal box.

OPERATING INFORMATION

Opening Times: 2025 Dates: 25th March then two Sundays each month until October, one for Diesel and one for Steam. Santa Specials operate on some dates during December.
Please check the website for further details.
Steam Working: Usually, the last Sunday in the month.
Prices: Adult Day Rover £15.00
Child Day Rover £10.00 (Ages 3 to 15)
Family Day Rover £35.00
(2 adults + 3 children)
All tickets offer unlimited rides on the day of issue and prices may vary on special event days.

Detailed Directions by Car::
From All Parts: Isfield is just off the A26 midway between Lewes and Uckfield.

Lincolnshire Wolds Railway

Address: The Railway Station, Station Road, Ludborough, DN36 5SQ
Telephone Nº: (01507) 363881
Year Formed: 1979
Gauge: Standard
Web: www.lincolnshirewoldsrailway.co.uk

Location of Line: Ludborough – just off the A16(T) between Grimsby and Louth
Length of Line: 1½ miles
Nº of Steam Locos: 5
Nº of Other Locos: 4
Approx Nº of Visitors P.A.: 10,000

GENERAL INFORMATION

Nearest Mainline Station: Grimsby (8 miles)
Nearest Bus Stop: Ludborough (½ mile)
Car Parking: Available at Ludborough Station only
Coach Parking: Space for 1 coach only
Souvenir Shop/Museum: Yes
Food & Drinks: Yes

SPECIAL INFORMATION

The LWR operates on a stretch of line which was once part of the Great Northern route from Boston to Grimsby. Heritage steam trains currently run between Ludborough and North Thoresby and work is now in progress to extend the line southwards towards Louth.

OPERATING INFORMATION

Opening Times: 2025 dates: 30th March; 21st April; 5th, 6th, 25th & 26th May; 8th, 15th & 22nd June; 5th, 13th, 20th & 27th July; 3rd, 6th, 10th, 13th, 17th, 20th, 24th, 25th, 27th & 31st August; 7th, 13th, 14th, 21st & 28th September; 12th & 26th October; 16th November. Santa Specials (advance booking essential) operate on 13th, 14th, 20th & 21st December.
Steam Working: All operating days
Prices: Adult Day Ticket £10.00
Child Day Ticket £6.00
Concession Day Ticket £8.00
Note: Single and Return Fares are cheaper

Detailed Directions by Car:
The Railway is situated near Ludborough, ½ mile off the A16(T) Louth to Grimsby road. Follow the brown tourist signs for ½ mile to Fulstow to reach the station. Do not turn into Ludborough but stay on the bypass.

LLANGOLLEN RAILWAY

Address: The Station, Abbey Road, Llangollen, Denbighshire LL20 8SN
Telephone Nº: (01978) 860979
Year Formed: 1975
Location of Line: Valley of the River Dee from Llangollen to Corwen
Length of Line: 10 miles

Nº of Steam Locos: 3
Nº of Other Locos: 6
Approx Nº of Visitors P.A.: 110,000
Gauge: Standard
Website: www.llangollen-railway.co.uk
E-mail: info@llangollen-railway.co.uk

GENERAL INFORMATION

Nearest Mainline Station: Ruabon (6 miles)
Nearest Bus Station: Wrexham (12 miles)
Car Parking: Llangollen Royal International Pavilion (SatNav post code: LL20 8SW)
Coach Parking: Market Street car park in town centre (SatNav post code: LL20 8PS)
Souvenir Shop(s): Yes – at Llangollen Station
Food & Drinks: Yes – at Llangollen and Carrog and also at Berwyn and Glyndyfrdwy on Gala Days

SPECIAL INFORMATION

The route originally formed part of the line from Ruabon to Barmouth Junction which closed in 1964.

The railway has been rebuilt by volunteers since 1975 and now runs 10 miles through to Corwen.

OPERATING INFORMATION

Opening Times: 2025 dates: Weekends from 15th February to 9th November as well as Easter Holiday Week. Daily except for non-Bank Holiday Mondays and Fridays from 6th May to 28th September. Santa Specials operate in December.
Steam Working: Most operating days
Prices: Adult Day Rover £27.50
                    Child Day Rover £12.00
                    Concession Day Rover £25.00
Note: Prices above are for online tickets. Return tickets are cheaper than Day Rovers.

Detailed Directions by Car:
From South & West: Go via the A5 to Llangollen. At the traffic lights turn into Castle Street to the River bridge; From North & East: Take the A483 to A539 junction and then via Trefor to Llangollen River bridge. The Station is adjacent to the River Dee.   SATNAV use LL20 8SN (but no parking available at the station).

Mangapps Railway Museum

Address: Southminster Road, Burnham-on-Crouch, Essex   CM0 8QG
Telephone Nº: (01621) 784898
Year Formed: 1989
Location of Line: Mangapps Farm
Length of Line: ¾ mile

Nº of Steam Locos: 2 (1 in service)
Nº of Other Locos: 10
Approx Nº of Visitors P.A.: 22,000
Gauge: Standard
Website: www.mangapps.co.uk

GENERAL INFORMATION

Nearest Mainline Station: Burnham-on-Crouch (1 mile)
Nearest Bus Station: –
Car Parking: Ample free parking at site
Coach Parking: Ample free parking at site
Souvenir Shop(s): Yes
Food & Drinks: Yes – drinks and snacks only

SPECIAL INFORMATION

The Railway endeavours to recreate the atmosphere of an East Anglian light railway. It also includes an extensive museum with an emphasis on East Anglian items and signalling.

OPERATING INFORMATION

Opening Times: 2025 dates: Closed during January and then open every weekend and Bank Holiday from the 1st February to 26th October, daily during School Holidays and for Santa Specials in December. Please contact the railway for details of opening times during the School Holidays and for any other information.
Steam Working: Please contact the railway for details of steam days.
Prices: Adults £15.00
   Children £8.00 (Under-3s ride for free)
   Concessions £15.00
Note: Prices for special event days may differ.

Detailed Directions by Car:
From South & West: From M25 take either the A12 or A127 and then the A130 to Rettendon Turnpike and then follow signs to Burnham; From North: From A12 take A414 to Oak Corner then follow signs to Burnham.

THE MIDDLETON RAILWAY

Address: The Station, Moor Road, Hunslet, Leeds LS10 2JQ
Year Formed: 1960
Location of Line: Moor Road to Middleton Park
Length of Line: 1½ miles

Nº of Steam Locos: 9
Nº of Other Locos: 4
Approx Nº of Visitors P.A.: 20,000
Gauge: Standard
Website: www.middletonrailway.org.uk
E-mail: info@middletonrailway.org.uk

GENERAL INFORMATION

Nearest Mainline Station: Leeds City (1 mile)
Nearest Bus Station: Leeds (1½ miles)
Car Parking: Free parking at site
Coach Parking: Free parking at site
Souvenir Shop(s): Yes
Food & Drinks: Yes

SPECIAL INFORMATION

The Middleton Railway is the oldest working railway in the world and was established in 1758 by Act of Parliament. The railway is also the first Standard Gauge line to be operated by volunteers and the first revenue-earning steam locomotive ran here in 1812. The railway also hosts a working museum housing a collection of Leeds built locomotives.

OPERATING INFORMATION

Opening Times: 2025 dates: Weekends, Bank Holidays and School Holidays from 5th April to the 5th October plus Santa Specials on weekends in December. Also open on Wednesdays in August. Services run approximately every 40 minutes from 10.30am to 3.30pm.
Steam Working: Diesels usually operate on Saturdays and on Wednesdays in August. All other services tend to be steam-hauled including Santa Specials in December.
Prices: Adult Day Rover £9.00
Child Day Rover £4.00
(Under-3s free of charge)
Family £22.00 (2 adult + 3 child)
Tickets provide for unlimited travel on the day of issue. For a full timetable and details of special events, please check the railway's website.
Note: Different prices may apply on Special Event days.

Detailed Directions by Car:
From the South: Take the M621 Northbound and exit at Junction 5. Turn right at the top of the slip road and take the 3rd exit at the roundabout. The Railway is 50 yards on the right; From the West: Take the M621 Southbound and exit at Junction 6. Turn left at the end of the slip road then left again into Moor Road at the next set of traffic lights. Bear right at the mini roundabout and the railway is on the left after 150 yards.

MID-HANTS RAILWAY (WATERCRESS LINE)

Address: The Railway Station, Alresford, Hampshire SO24 9JG
Telephone Nº: (01962) 733810
Year Formed: 1977
Location of Line: Alresford to Alton
Length of Line: 10 miles

Nº of Steam Locos: 17
Nº of Other Locos: 5 + 1 DEMU
Approx Nº of Visitors P.A.: 120,000
Gauge: Standard
Website: www.watercressline.co.uk
E-mail: info@watercressline.co.uk

GENERAL INFORMATION

Nearest Mainline Station: Alton (adjacent) or Winchester (7 miles)
Nearest Bus Station: Winchester or Alton
Car Parking: Pay and display at Alton and Alresford Stations (Alresford free on Sundays & Bank Holidays)
Coach Parking: By arrangement at Alresford Station
Souvenir Shop(s): At Alresford, Ropley & Alton
Food & Drinks: Yes – Buffet on most trains. 'West Country' buffet at Alresford

SPECIAL INFORMATION

As the name implies the area was the centre of watercress-growing in the UK, with Alresford Station being the place from which huge quantities of watercress were once despatched.

OPERATING INFORMATION

Opening Times: 2025 dates: Weekends, Wednesdays, Thursdays and School Holidays from 5th March to the 2nd June then daily throughout July, August and September.
Please check the website for full details of Summer working and Santa Specials.
Steam Working: All operating days although a Steam/DMU combination is sometimes in service.
Prices: Adult £28.00
Child £14.00 (Under-5s travel free)
Family £56.00 to £78.00
(depends on number of family members)
Prices shown allow unlimited travel on the day of purchase. Prices may differ on Special Event days. A discount is available for pre-booked online tickets.

Detailed Directions by Car:
From the East: Take the M25 then A3 and A31 to Alton; From the West: Exit the M3 at Junction 9 and take the A31 to Alresford Station.

Mid-Norfolk Railway

Address: The Railway Station, Station Road, Dereham NR19 1DF
Telephone Nº: (01362) 690633
Year Formed: 1995
Location: East Dereham to Wymondham
Length of Line: 11 miles

Nº of Steam Locos: 1 + visiting locos
Nº of Other Locos: 9
Approx Nº of Visitors P.A.: 16,000
Gauge: Standard
Website: www.midnorfolkrailway.co.uk
E-mail: info@mnr.org.uk

GENERAL INFORMATION

Nearest Mainline Station: Wymondham (1 mile)
Nearest Bus Station: Wymondham or East Dereham – each ½ mile away
Car Parking: Available at Dereham Station
Coach Parking: Available at Dereham Station
Souvenir Shop(s): Yes – at Dereham Station
Food & Drinks: Yes – at Dereham Station

SPECIAL INFORMATION

The Mid-Norfolk Railway aims to preserve the former Great Eastern Railway from Wymondham to County School. The section from Wymondham to Dereham was opened to passenger and freight traffic in May 1999 and clearance work is now complete on the East Dereham to County School section.

OPERATING INFORMATION

Opening Times: 2025 dates: Weekends and Bank Holidays from the 1st March to 19th October. Also open on most Wednesdays, Thursdays & Fridays from April to the 26th September. The Polar Express train rides run on dates in November and December.
Steam Working: Please check the website for details
Prices: Adult Day Rover £19.95
Child Day Rover £7.00
Senior Citizen Day Rover £18.00
Note: First Class tickets are also available and lower prices apply at off-peak times.

Detailed Directions by Car:
From All Parts: From the A47 bypass, turn into Dereham and follow the signs for the Town Centre. Turn right at the BP Garage – look out for the brown tourist signs – you will see the Station on your right.

Mid-Suffolk Light Railway Museum

Address: Brockford Station, Wetheringsett, Suffolk   IP14 5PW
Telephone Nº: (01449) 766874
Year Formed: 1991
Location of Line: Wetheringsett, Suffolk
Length of Line: ¼ mile (being extended)

Nº of Steam Locos: 3
Nº of Other Locos: 2
Approx Nº of Visitors P.A.: 6,000
Gauge: Standard
Website: www.mslr.org.uk
E-mail: marketing@mslr.org.uk

GENERAL INFORMATION

Nearest Mainline Station: Stowmarket
Nearest Bus Station: Ipswich
Car Parking: Available on site
Coach Parking: Available by prior arrangement
Souvenir Shop(s): Yes
Food & Drinks: Yes

SPECIAL INFORMATION

The Mid-Suffolk Light Railway served the heart of the county for 50 years, despite being bankrupt before the first train ran. In a beautiful rural setting, the Museum seeks to preserve the memory of a unique branch line. Early in 2023 a track extension to Aspall Halt station was completed and work on constructing the station itself is now in progress.

OPERATING INFORMATION

Opening Times: 2025 dates: 20th & 21st April; 25th & 26th May; 8th, 15th, 22nd & 29th June; 6th, 12th, 13th, 20th & 27th July; 3rd, 10th, 17th, 24th, 25th & 31st August. Please check the website for later events including Santa Specials in December.
Steam Working: All operational days.
Please contact the railway or check the website for further information.
Prices: Adult £12.00   Child £6.00 (Under-5s free)
   Family Ticket £30.00   Concession £10.00
Tickets allow unlimited travel on the day of issue and act as season tickets for the calendar year (subject to conditions). Special Event days have higher prices.

Detailed Directions by Car:
The Museum is situated 14 miles north of Ipswich and 28 miles south of Norwich, just off the A140. Look for Mendlesham TV mast and then follow the brown tourist signs from the A140.

MIDLAND RAILWAY – BUTTERLEY

Address: Butterley Station, Ripley, Derbyshire   DE5 3QZ
Telephone Nº: (01773) 570140
Year Formed: 1969
Location of Line: Butterley, near Ripley
Length of Line: Standard gauge 3½ miles, Narrow gauge 0.8 mile

Nº of Steam Locos: 13
Nº of Other Locos: 20
Approx Nº of Visitors P.A.: 100,000
Gauge: Standard, various Narrow gauges and miniature
Web: www.midlandrailway-butterley.co.uk

GENERAL INFORMATION

Nearest Mainline Station: Alfreton (6 miles)
Nearest Bus Station: Bus stop outside Butterley Station.
Car Parking: Free parking at site – ample space
Coach Parking: Free parking at site
Souvenir Shop(s): Yes – at Butterley and Swanwick
Food & Drinks: Yes – both sites + bar on train

SPECIAL INFORMATION

The Railway is a unique project with a huge Museum development together with narrow gauge, miniature & model railways as well as a country park. Includes an Award-winning Victorian Railwayman's church and Princess Royal Class Locomotive Trust Depot.

OPERATING INFORMATION

Opening Times: 2025 dates: Trains run on weekends and Bank Holidays from 5th April to 28th September and also on Wednesdays during the School Holidays. Santa Specials run on weekends in December. Please check the website for further information. Open from 9.30am to 4.30pm.
Steam Working: Please check the website or phone (01773) 570140 for details.
Prices: Adults £12.00 to £16.00
            Children £6.00 to £8.00 (Ages 5 to 15)
            Concessions £11.00 to £15.00
            Family £30.00 to £40.00
Prices vary depend on the event being run.

Detailed Directions by Car:
From All Parts: From the M1 exit at Junction 28 and take the A38 towards Derby. The Railway is signposted at the junction with the B6179.

MOUNTSORREL RAILWAY MUSEUM

Address: 240 Swithland Lane, Mountsorrel, LE7 7UE
Telephone Nº: (0116) 237 4591
Year Formed: 2007 (opened 2015)
Location: Swithland Sidings & Nunckley Hill Quarry, Mountsorrel.
Length of Line: Short demo line only

Nº of Steam Locos: 1
Nº of Other Locos: 1
Approx Nº of Visitors P.A.: Not known
Gauge: Standard & 2 Foot
Website: www.heritage-centre.co.uk

GENERAL INFORMATION

Nearest Mainline Station: Loughborough (1¾ mile)
Nearest Bus Station: Loughborough
Car Parking: Available on site
Coach Parking: Available on site
Food & Drinks: Granite Coffee Shop (free entry)

SPECIAL INFORMATION

The Heritage Centre and Museum occupy a location at the end of the 1¼ mile Mountsorrel Branch Line which is operated by the Great Central Railway at Loughborough.

OPERATING INFORMATION

Opening Times: 2025 dates: Open daily from 10.00am to 4.45pm. Please check the website for details of Special Events.
Steam Working: None at present
Prices: Adult £2.00
Child £1.00 (Ages 2 to 15)
Note: Prices shown are for entry to both the Centre and the Museum.

Detailed Directions by Car:
Take the Southbound A6 from Loughborough and exit after 4½ miles into Granite Way. Continue into Mountsorrel, turn left at the roundabout onto Loughborough Road, then right at the second roundabout onto The Green. Continue into Rothley Road, turn right into Halstead Road and continue to the end of the road before turning right into Swithland Lane. The Heritage Centre is a short distance along on the left.

Nene Valley Railway

Address: Wansford Station, Stibbington, Peterborough PE8 6LR
Telephone Nº: (01780) 784444
E-mail: nvrorg@nvr.org.uk
Year Formed: 1977
Location: Off A1 to west of Peterborough
Length of Line: 7½ miles

Nº of Steam Locos: 15
Nº of Other Locos: 7
Approx Nº of Visitors P.A.: 65,000
Gauge: Standard
Website: www.nvr.org.uk
E-mail: Contact via the website

GENERAL INFORMATION

Nearest Mainline Station: Peterborough (¾ mile)
Nearest Bus Station: Peterborough (Queensgate – ¾ mile)
Car Parking: Free parking at Wansford & Orton Mere
Coach Parking: Free coach parking at Wansford
Souvenir Shop(s): Yes
Food & Drinks: Yes – at Wansford and Overton

SPECIAL INFORMATION

The railway is truly international in flavour with British and Continental locomotives and rolling stock.

OPERATING INFORMATION

Opening Times: 2025 dates: Most weekends and Bank Holidays from 22nd March to 2nd November. Also open on most Wednesdays from 9th April to 24th September, most Thursdays in the School summer holidays and at various other times. Santa Specials run on dates in November & December. Please contact the Railway for further details. Trains run from 10.00am to as late as 5.15pm, depending on the time of the year.
Steam Working: Most services are steam hauled apart from on diesel days and times of high fire risk.
Prices: Adult Day Rover £19.00
　　　　　Child Day Rover £10.00 (Under-3s free)
　　　　　Family £52.00 (2 adults + 3 children)
Note: Pre-booked tickets and railcar fares are cheaper.

Detailed Directions by Car:
The railway is situated off the southbound carriageway of the A1 between the A47 and A605 junctions – west of Peterborough and south of Stamford.

NORTH NORFOLK RAILWAY (THE POPPY LINE)

Address: Sheringham Station, Sheringham, Norfolk NR26 8RA
Telephone Nº: (01263) 820800
E-mail: enquiries@nnrailway.co.uk
Year Formed: 1975
Location of Line: Sheringham to Holt via Weybourne

Length of Line: 5½ miles
Nº of Steam Locos: 9 (+ visiting locos)
Nº of Other Locos: 6
Approx Nº of Visitors P.A.: 166,000
Gauge: Standard
Website: www.nnrailway.co.uk
E-mail: enquiries@nnrailway.co.uk

GENERAL INFORMATION

Nearest Mainline Station: Sheringham (200 yards)
Nearest Bus Station: Outside the Station
Car and Coach Parking:
Adjacent to Sheringham and Holt
Souvenir Shop(s): Available at all stations
Food & Drinks: Yes – main catering facilities at Sheringham Station. Light refreshments elsewhere.

SPECIAL INFORMATION

Lunch and evening dinner trains are scheduled throughout the year. Please check the website for times and fares. Weybourne Station is licensed for weddings.

OPERATING INFORMATION

Opening Times: 2025 dates: Sundays from 16th February to 30th March then most days from 5th April to 2nd November except for Mondays and Fridays in April, May, June, September and October. Santa Specials run during December and other Special Events are held throughout the year. Please check the railway's website for further details.
Steam Working: 9.55am to 5.00pm (during high season)
Prices: Adult £23.50
 Child £16.45   (Under-3s travel free)
 Family £68.00   (2 adults + 2 children)
 Family £79.50   (2 adults + 3 children)
 Dogs and Bicycles £3.00 each
The prices shown above are for all-day, hop-on, hop-off, Day Rover tickets purchased on the day. Special Events may have different prices and pre-booked tickets are cheaper.

Detailed Directions by Car:
Sheringham Station is situated just off the A149. Holt Station is located at High Kelling, just off the A148.

NORTH YORKSHIRE MOORS RAILWAY

Address: 12 Park Street, Pickering, North Yorkshire YO18 7AJ
Telephone Nº: (01751) 472508 (enquiries)
Year Formed: 1967
Location of Line: Pickering to Grosmont via stations at Levisham and Goathland
Length of Line: 18 miles

Nº of Steam Locos: 16
Nº of Other Locos: 10
Approx Nº of Visitors P.A.: 350,000
Gauge: Standard
Website: www.nymr.co.uk
E-mail: info@nymr.co.uk

GENERAL INFORMATION

Nearest Mainline Station: Grosmont or Whitby
Nearest Bus Station: Pickering (½ mile)
Car Parking: Available at each station
Coach Parking: None
Souvenir Shop(s): Yes – at Pickering, Goathland, and Grosmont Stations plus Grosmont MPD
Food & Drinks: Pickering, Grosmont & Goathland. Also at Levisham on weekends and bank holidays.

SPECIAL INFORMATION

The NYMR runs through the spectacular North York Moors National Park and is the most popular heritage railway in the country. As seen in 'Heartbeat' and the first Harry Potter film. The railway operates extended services to and from Whitby.

OPERATING INFORMATION

Opening Times: 2025 dates: Open daily from 31st March to 2nd November. Santa Specials operate on weekends in December and a Winter timetable operates thereafter so please check the website for this information when it becomes available.
Steam Working: All services except during periods of excessive heat and drought when Diesel power may be required to prevent wildfires.
Prices: Adult Day Rover £49.50 to £54.50
                Child Day Rover £12.15 to £13.50
                   (Ages 4 to 15 years)
                Family Day Rover £99.00 to £110.00
Note: The higher prices shown above include a donation to the railway.

Detailed Directions by Car:
From the South: Follow the A64 past York to the Malton bypass then take the A169 to Pickering; From the North: Take A171 towards Whitby then follow the minor road through Egton to Grosmont.

NORTHAMPTON & LAMPORT RAILWAY

Address: Pitsford & Bramford Station, Pitsford Road, Chapel Brampton, Northampton   NN6 8BA
Telephone Nº: (01604) 820327 (infoline)
Year Formed: 1983 (became operational in November 1995)
Length of Line: 2 miles

Nº of Steam Locos: 8
Nº of Other Locos: 4
Approx Nº of Visitors P.A.: 9,300
Gauge: Standard
Website: www.nlr.org.uk
E-mail: enquiries@nlr.org.uk

GENERAL INFORMATION

Nearest Mainline Station: Northampton (5 miles)
Nearest Bus Station: Northampton (5 miles)
Car Parking: Free parking at site
Coach Parking: Free parking at site
Souvenir Shop(s): Yes
Food & Drinks: Yes

SPECIAL INFORMATION

The railway operates on a section of the old London & North Western Railway line between Northampton and Market Harborough and became operational again on 18th November 1995. In 2024 the line was extended to Boughton Station.

OPERATING INFORMATION

Opening Times: 2025 dates: Most Sundays and Bank holidays from 30th March until 7th September and Santa Specials on most weekends in December. Open from 10.30am to 4.30pm (the last train runs at 3.30pm). Please contact the railway for a more detailed timetable.
Steam Working: Bank Holiday weekends and Santa Specials in December. Also on some other Event Days but please check website for full details.
Prices: Adult £8.00
 Child £7.00 (Under-2s ride free)
 Concessions £7.00
 Family £23.50 (2 adults + 2 children)
Fares may may be more on Special Event days and Day Rover Tickets are also more expensive.

Detailed Directions by Car:
The station is situated along the Pitsford road at Chapel Brampton, approximately 5 miles north of Northampton. Heading north out of town, it is signposted to the right on the A5199 (A50) Welford Road at Chapel Brampton crossroads or on the left on the A508 Market Harborough road at the Pitsford turn.

Northants. Ironstone Railway Trust

Address: Hunsbury Hill Museum, Hunsbury Hill Country Park, West Hunsbury, Northampton NN4 9UW
Telephone Nº: (01604) 702031
Year Formed: 1974
Gauge: Standard
Website: www.northantsirinstonerailway.co.uk
E-mail: info@northantsirinstonerailway.co.uk

Location of Line: Hunsbury Hill Country Park, Northampton
Length of Line: Two-thirds of a mile
Nº of Steam Locos: 2 (1 operational)
Nº of Other Locos: 6 (2 operational)
Approx Nº of Visitors P.A.: Not known

GENERAL INFORMATION

Nearest Mainline Station: Northampton (2½ miles)
Nearest Bus Station: Northampton (3 miles)
Car Parking: Large free car park at the site
Coach Parking: Available at the site on request
Souvenir Shop(s): Yes
Food & Drinks: Yes

SPECIAL INFORMATION

The Railway has recently re-opened after a major rebuild and now operates along two-thirds of a mile of track. The Museum is dedicated to the Ironstone industry of Northamptonshire.

OPERATING INFORMATION

Opening Times: The museum is open during Easter weekend, Spring Bank Holiday weekend then the first Sunday of the month from June to October and also on other Bank Holidays throughout the year. Trains run at these times also. There may also be a number of special events throughout the year (including Santa Specials) – please contact the railway for further information.
Steam Working: An hourly service runs between 11.00am and 5.00pm.
Prices: Adult £6.50   Child £4.00
Admission to the museum and site is free of charge but donations are always welcome.

Detailed Directions by Car:
Exit the M1 at Junction 15A, and follow the road for approximately ½ mile. Turn left onto the A43 and after approximately 1 mile take the 3rd exit at the roundabout onto Danes Camp Way (A45). After ½ mile take the 4th exit at the roundabout onto Hunsbury Hill Road. Continue over two mini-roundabouts past the Rose & Claret Public House. The entrance to Hunsbury Hill Country Park for the railway is on the left.

PEAK RAIL PLC

Address: Matlock Station, Matlock, Derbyshire   DE4 3NA
Telephone Nº: 07979-496488
Year Formed: 1975
Location: Matlock to Rowsley South
Length of Line: Approximately 4½ miles

Nº of Steam Locos: 4
Nº of Other Locos: 40+
Approx Nº of Visitors P.A.: 150,000
Gauge: Standard
Website: www.peakrail.co.uk
E-mail: peakrail@peakrail.co.uk

GENERAL INFORMATION

Nearest Mainline Station: Matlock
Nearest Bus Station: Matlock
Car Parking: Paid car parking at Matlock Station. 200 free parking spaces available at Rowsley South Station and 20 free spaces at Darley Dale Station
Coach Parking: Free parking at Rowsley South
Souvenir Shop(s): Yes
Food & Drinks: Yes – R.M.B. Buffet on the train and the Rowsley Buffet at Rowsley South Station.

SPECIAL INFORMATION

The Palatine Restaurant Car is often available whilst travelling on the train, catering for Sunday Lunches, Teas and Party Bookings (please check with the Railway for operating dates for the Palatine). Coach parties are welcomed when the railway is operating.

OPERATING INFORMATION

Opening Times: 2025 dates: Weekends, Bank Holidays and School Holidays throughout the year from 15th February to 2nd November. Also Wednesdays from 17th May to 24th September and Thursdays in August. Santa Specials run during weekends in December.
Steam Working: All services throughout the year.
Prices: Adult £15.00
 Children (Ride free with a paying adult)
 Concessions £13.00
Note: Tickets allow unlimited travel on the day of purchase but Special Events are more expensive.

Detailed Directions by Car:
Exit the M1 at Junctions 28, 29 or 30 and follow signs towards Matlock. From North and South take A6 direct to Matlock. From Stoke-on-Trent, take the A52 to Ashbourne, then the A5035 to Matlock. Upon reaching Matlock follow the brown tourist signs.

Plym Valley Railway

Address: Marsh Mills Station, Coypool Road, Plympton, Plymouth   PL7 4NW
Telephone Nº: (01752) 345078
Year Formed: 1980
Location of Line: Marsh Mills to Plym Bridge Platform
Length of Line: 1½ miles

Nº of Steam Locos: 4
Nº of Other Locos: 4
Approx Nº of Visitors P.A.: 5,000
Gauge: Standard
Website: www.plymrail.co.uk
E-mail: plymvalleyrailway@gmail.com

GENERAL INFORMATION

Nearest Mainline Station: Plymouth (4 miles)
Nearest Bus Station: Plymouth (3 miles)
Car Parking: Available at the Park & Ride opposite the main gates to the railway
Coach Parking: As above
Souvenir Shop(s): Yes
Food & Drinks: Light snacks available

SPECIAL INFORMATION

2012 saw the opening of the extension of the line to Plym Bridge. This is a section of the former Great Western branch line which from Tavistock Junction through to Launceston. The railway now plans to further develop their visitor facilities at Marsh Mills.

OPERATING INFORMATION

Opening Times: 2025 dates: Open 11.00am to 5.00pm on most Sundays from 16th March to 2nd November and brake van rides are usually available when full passenger services do not run. Please check the website for details of the services on other dates which include every Saturday in August and Santa Specials in December.
Steam Working: Contact the railway for details.
Prices: Adult Return £8.00   Day Rover £12.00
Child Return £4.00   Day Rover £6.00
Family Return £20.00
Note: There is no charge to visit the station. Higher prices are charged for Special Events which may need to be pre-booked.

Detailed Directions by Car:
Leave the A38 at the Marsh Mills turn-off and take the B3416 towards Plympton. Turn left into Coypool Road just after the McDonalds restaurant. From Plymouth City Centre, take the A374 to Marsh Mills, then as above.

Pontypool & Blaenavon Railway

Address: 33 Broad Street, Blaenavon, Torfaen   NP4 9NF
Telephone Nº: (01495) 792263 (Shop)
Year Formed: 1980 (Opened 1983)
Location of Line: Just off the B4248 between Blaenavon and Brynmawr
Length of Line: 3½ miles

Nº of Steam Locos: 2
Nº of Other Locos: 1
Approx Nº of Visitors P.A.: 16,500
Gauge: Standard
Website: www.bhrailway.co.uk
E-mail: info@bhrailway.co.uk

GENERAL INFORMATION

Nearest Mainline Station: Abergavenny (5 miles)
Nearest Bus Station: Blaenavon Town (1½ miles) – regular bus service within ¼ mile (except Sundays)
Car Parking: Free parking for 50 cars on site
Coach Parking: Available on site
Souvenir Shop(s): Yes – at Furness Sidings Station and also a shop at 33 Broad Street, Blaenavon
Food & Drinks: Light refreshments on the train and at the station.

SPECIAL INFORMATION

The railway operates over very steep gradients and is the highest standard gauge preserved railway in England and Wales.

OPERATING INFORMATION

Opening Times: 2025 dates: Every weekend and Bank Holiday Monday from 22nd March to 5th October plus some Wednesdays in August and September, Halloween Trains between 25th & 31st October and Santa Specials in December. Please check the website for further details.
Steam Working: Trains are steam-hauled during Peak days and Special Steam Days during May and June. Diesel locos may be used on quiet days. Please contact the Railway for further information.
Prices: Adult Day Rover £16.00
    Child Day Rover £8.00 (Under-3s free)
    Family Day Rover £40.00 (2 adult + 2 child)
Note: Tickets bought in advance are cheaper.

Detailed Directions by Car:

From All Parts: The railway is situated just off the B4248 between Blaenavon and Brynmawr and is well signposted as you approach Blaenavon. Use Junction 25A if using the M4 from the East, or Junction 26 from the West. Head for Pontypool. From the Midlands use the M50, A40 then A465 to Brynmawr. From North & West Wales consider using the 'Heads of the Valleys' A465 to Brynmawr. As you approach the Railway, look out for the Colliery water tower – you can't miss it!

Ribble Steam Railway

Address: Chain Caul Road, Preston, PR2 2PD
Telephone N°: (01772) 728800
Year Formed: 2005
Location: West of Preston City Centre
Length of Line: 3 mile round trip

N° of Steam Locos: 37
N° of Other Locos: 20
Approx N° of Visitors P.A.: 20,000+
Gauge: Standard
Website: www.ribblesteam.org.uk
E-mail: enquiries@ribblesteam.org.uk

GENERAL INFORMATION

Nearest Mainline Station: Preston (2 miles)
Nearest Bus Station: Preston (2 miles)
Car Parking: Available on site
Coach Parking: Available on site
Souvenir Shop(s): Yes
Food & Drinks: Available

SPECIAL INFORMATION

The line traverses a swing bridge across the Marina entrance – the only preserved steam line in Britain to have such a feature! The railway also has the largest collection of standard gauge industrial locomotives housed under cover in the UK.

OPERATING INFORMATION

Opening Times: 2025 dates: Every Saturday from 5th April to 27th September plus Bank Holiday Weekends and some other dates for Halloween and Santa Specials.
Please check the website for full details.
Steam Working: On all days when the railway is open to the public. Trains run hourly from 11.00am to 4.00pm.
Prices: Adult Return £12.50
Child Return £7.50 (Under-3s ride free)
Concessionary Return £10.00
Family Return £32.00
Note: Higher prices apply on Special Event days. Please contact the railway for further information.

Detailed Directions by Car:
From All Parts: The Railway is located on the Riversway/Docklands Business and Residential Park, just off the A583 Lytham/Blackpool road and approximately 1½ miles to the west of Preston City Centre. Follow the Brown Tourist signs from the A583 for the railway.

Rocks by Rail – The Living Ironstone Museum

Address: Ashwell Road, Cottesmore, Oakham, Rutland LE15 7FF
Telephone N°: 07974 171068
Year Formed: 1979
Location of Line: Between the villages of Cottesmore and Ashwell
Length of Line: ¾ mile

N° of Steam Locos: 12
N° of Other Locos: 12
Approx N° of Visitors P.A.: 8,000
Gauge: Standard
Website: www.rocks-by-rail.org
E-mail: curator@rocks-by-rail.org

GENERAL INFORMATION

Nearest Mainline Station: Oakham (4 miles)
Nearest Bus Station: Cottesmore/Ashwell (1½ miles)
Car Parking: Available at the site
Coach Parking: Limited space available
Souvenir Shop(s): None
Food & Drinks: Available on Thursdays and many Sundays from Easter to October.

SPECIAL INFORMATION

Rocks by Rail is a Museum based within 19 acres of reclaimed Limestone Quarry.

OPERATING INFORMATION

Opening Times: 2025 dates: Static viewing on Tuesdays and Thursdays from 10.00am to 4.00pm and most Sundays from 20th April to 19th October. Services operate on 20th, 21st & 27th April; 4th, 5th, 8th, 11th, 25th & 26th May; 15th & 19th June; 13th & 27th July; 6th, 15th, 24th & 25th August; 7th & 21st September and 5th & 19th October.
Steam Working: Brake Van rides on Some Sundays. Please contact the railway for further details.
Prices: Adults £10.00   Children £6.00 (age 3-14)
  Concessions £8.00
  Family Ticket £25.00 (2 adults + 3 children)
  (Above prices are for Steam Days)

Detailed Directions by Car:
From All Parts: The Museum is situated 4 miles north of Oakham between Ashwell and Cottesmore. Follow the brown tourist signs from the B668 Oakham to A1 road or the signs from the A606 Stamford to Oakham Road.

ROYAL DEESIDE RAILWAY

Address: Milton of Crathes, Crathes, Banchory   AB31 5QH
Telephone Nº: (01330) 844416
Year Formed: 1996
Location of Line: Milton of Crathes
Length of Line: 1 mile

Nº of Steam Locos: 3
Nº of Other Locos: 3 + 1 BMU
Approx Nº of Visitors P.A.: 12,000
Gauge: Standard
Website: www.deeside-railway.co.uk
E-mail: info@deeside-railway.co.uk

GENERAL INFORMATION

Nearest Mainline Station: Aberdeen (14 miles)
Nearest Bus Station: Stagecoach Bluebird bus stop nearby on A93.
Car Parking: Free parking available on site
Coach Parking: Free parking available on site
Souvenir Shop(s): Yes
Food & Drinks: Yes – inside the restored Victorian station and also inside a static catering car.

SPECIAL INFORMATION

The line is gradually being extended to Banchory and, when completed, will be 2 miles in length.

OPERATING INFORMATION

Opening Times: 2025 dates: Most Sundays from 30th March to 26th October plus Santa Specials on the last weekend in November and each weekend in December. Please contact the railway for further information.
Steam Working: Please contact the railway for details of steaming dates.
Prices: Adult Day Rover £8.00
Child Day Rover £4.00 (Under-3s free)
Senior Citizen Day Rover £6.00
Family Day Rover Ticket £20.00
(2 adults + 3 children)

Detailed Directions by Car:
From the South: Take the A90 to Stonehaven. Exit onto the B979 for Stonehaven and follow into the town square. Turn left at the traffic lights and follow signs for the A957 to Banchory (Historic Slug Road). Follow this road for 14 mile via Durris to Crathes and the junction with the A93. Turn left and follow the Brown Tourist signs, turning left for the railway after approximately 600 yards; From the North & West: Follow the A980 to Banchory and turn left onto the A93. Turn right following the Brown Tourist signs for the railway.

RUSHDEN TRANSPORT MUSEUM & RAILWAY

Address: Rushden Station, Station Approach, Rushden, NN10 0AW
Telephone N° 0300-3023150
Year Formed: 1985
Location of Line: Rushden, Northants.
Length of Line: ½ mile (each paid trip is 2½ miles in distance)

N° of Steam Locos: 3 (All under repair)
N° of Other Locos: 5
Approx N° of Visitors P.A.: 5,000
Gauge: Standard
Website: www.rhts.co.uk
E-mail: secretary@rhts.co.uk

GENERAL INFORMATION

Nearest Mainline Station: Wellingborough (5 miles)
Nearest Bus Station: Northampton (14 miles)
Car Parking: Available on site. On operating days a nearby public car park must be used.
Coach Parking: None
Souvenir Shop(s): Yes
Food & Drinks: Available on operating weekends

SPECIAL INFORMATION

The Rushden Transport Museum is situated in the old Midland Railway Station of 1894 which once formed part of the Wellingborough to Higham Ferrers branch line. Taken over by the Rushden Historical Transport Society in 1984 the station also provides the society with a social club.

OPERATING INFORMATION

Opening Times: The Museum is open on Saturdays from the 30th March until the end of October (2.00pm to 4.00pm) and also on other Event Days. Please check the website for full details.
Steam Working: No Steam Working at present but a Class 142 'Pacer' Diesel Unit giving rides to visitors is operated by The Rushden, Higham & Wellingborough Railway.
Prices: A flat rate of £5.00 per ride is charged.

Detailed Directions by Car:
From All Parts: Take the A6 to the Rushden Bypass (to the south of the A45) and turn into John Clark Way by the large grey warehouses. The Station is located on the right-hand side of the road after approximately 400 yards.

SEVERN VALLEY RAILWAY

Correspondence Address:
1 Comberton Place,
Kidderminster   DY10 1QR
Telephone Nº: (01562) 757900
Year Formed: 1965
Location of Line: Kidderminster (Worcs.) to Bridgnorth (Shropshire)
Length of Line: 16 miles

Nº of Steam Locos: 27 (7 in service)
Nº of Other Locos: 16
Approx Nº of Passengers P.A.: 250,000
Gauge: Standard
Website: www.svr.co.uk
E-mail: contact@svr.co.uk

GENERAL INFORMATION

Nearest Mainline Station: Kidderminster (adjacent)
Nearest Bus Station: Kidderminster (500 yards)
Car Parking: Large car park at Kidderminster. Spaces also available at other stations.
Coach Parking: At Kidderminster
Souvenir Shop(s): At Kidderminster & Bridgnorth
Food & Drinks: On most trains. Also at Bewdley, Bridgnorth, Kidderminster and The Engine House

SPECIAL INFORMATION

The SVR has numerous special events details of which can be found on the website. 'The Engine House', the railway's visitor and education centre, is a further attraction at Highley.

OPERATING INFORMATION

Opening Times: 2025 dates: Weekends from 15th February to 2nd November plus most Wednesdays, Thursdays and Bank Holidays for most of May, June and July as well during the School Holidays. Please check the website for further details.
Steam Working: Train times vary depending on timetable information, details. on website.
Prices: Adult £33.00
   Child £22.00 (Under-4s ride free)
   Family Tickets £55.00 to £88.00
         (depends on numbers in family)
Note: Prices shown are for 'Freedom of Line' tickets purchased on the day of travel but advance bookings are cheaper.

Detailed Directions by Car:
For Kidderminster exit the M5 at Junction 3 or Junction 6 and follow the brown tourist signs for the railway; From the South: Take the M40 then M42 to Junction 1 for the A448 to Kidderminster.   SATNAV DY10 1QX

Somerset & Dorset Railway

Address: The Station, Silver Street, Midsomer Norton, BA3 2EY
Telephone Nº: (01761) 411221
Year Formed: 2019
Location of Line: Midsomer Norton
Length of Line: About 1 mile

Nº of Steam Locos: 1
Nº of Other Locos: 2
Approx Nº of Visitors P.A.: not known
Gauge: Standard
Website: www.sdjr.co.uk
E-mail: general@sdjr.co.uk

GENERAL INFORMATION

Nearest Mainline Station: Frome (10 miles)
Car Parking: Available opposite the railway at Norton Hill School (Postcode BA3 4AD)
Coach Parking: None
Souvenir Shop(s): None
Food & Drinks: None

SPECIAL INFORMATION

The Railway, which operates from Midsomer Norton Station along the old trackbed southwards towards Chilcompton, commenced operations during 2019.

OPERATING INFORMATION

Opening Times: 2025 dates: Most Sundays, Bank Holidays and some Wednesdays from 6th April to 2nd November plus weekends in December for 'Santa at the Station'.
Steam Working: Please check the website for further details.
Prices: Adult Rover £10.00
Child Rover £5.00 (Under-4s ride free)
Note: Additional charges may apply on Special Event days.

Detailed Directions by Car:
The Railway is located in Midsomer Norton at the side of the B3355 road, 400 yards to the south of the Town.

SOUTH DEVON RAILWAY

Address: The Station, Dartbridge Road
Buckfastleigh, Devon   TQ11 0DZ
Telephone Nº: 01364 644370
Year Formed: 1969
Location of Line: Totnes to Buckfastleigh via Staverton
Length of Line: 7 miles

Nº of Steam Locos: 15 (4 in service)
Nº of Other Locos: 11
Approx Nº of Visitors P.A.: 100,000+
Gauge: Standard
Website: www.southdevonrailway.co.uk
E-mail: trains@southdevonrailway.org

GENERAL INFORMATION

Nearest Mainline Station: Totnes (¼ mile)
Nearest Bus Station: Totnes (½ mile), Buckfastleigh (Station Road)
Car Parking: Free parking at Buckfastleigh and Council and National Rail parking at Totnes
Coach Parking: As above
Souvenir Shop(s): Yes – at Buckfastleigh
Food & Drinks: Yes – at Buckfastleigh & on train

SPECIAL INFORMATION

The railway was opened in 1872 as the Totnes, Buckfastleigh & Ashburton Railway.

OPERATING INFORMATION

Opening Times: 2025 dates: Most days from 5th April to 2nd November. Polar Express rides also run on weekends and some other dates during November and December.
Please contact the railway for further details.
Steam Working: Almost all trains are steam hauled.
Prices: Adult Return £22.00
　　　　　　Child Return £11.00 (Under-3s ride free)
　　　　　　Family Return £59.00 (2 Adult + 2 Child)
　　　　　　Family Return £40.00 (1 Adult + 2 Child)
　　　　　　Concession Return £21.00
Note: Extra discounts are available for large groups and 'Full-line Ranger Tickets' are also available.

Detailed Directions by Car:
Buckfastleigh is half way between Exeter and Plymouth on the A38 Devon Expressway. Totnes can be reached by taking the A385 from Paignton and Torquay. Brown tourist signs give directions for the railway.

SPA VALLEY RAILWAY

Address: West Station, Nevill Terrace, Tunbridge Wells, TN2 5QY
Telephone Nº: (01892) 300141
Year Formed: 1985
Location of Line: Tunbridge Wells West to Groombridge and Eridge
Length: 5 miles

Nº of Steam Locos: 10 (3 in service)
Nº of Other Locos: 10 + 3 DMUs
Approx Nº of Visitors P.A.: 42,000
Gauge: Standard
Website: www.spavalleyrailway.co.uk
E-mail: enquiries@spavalleyrailway.co.uk

GENERAL INFORMATION

Nearest Mainline Station: Eridge (cross-platform interchange with the mainline)
Nearest Bus Stop: Outside Sainsbury's (100yds)
Car Parking: Available in Tunbridge Wells nearby in Major Yorks Road, Union House & Linden Close
Coach Parking: Montacute Road (150 yards)
Souvenir Shop(s): Yes
Food & Drinks: Yes

SPECIAL INFORMATION

The Railway's Tunbridge Wells Terminus is in a historic and unique L.B. & S.C.R. engine shed. The extension to Eridge is now open at weekends and on public holidays and tickets inclusive of entry to Groombridge Place Gardens are also available.

OPERATING INFORMATION

Opening Times: 2025 dates: Weekends and Bank Holidays from 1st February to 26th October inclusive. Also open on Wednesdays and Thursdays from 23rd July to 28th August.
Trains usualluy operate from 10.20am to 3.20pm though this may vary on Special Event days.
Prices: Adult Return £16.00
   Child Return £9.00
   Concession Return £15.00
   Family Return £41.00 (2 adult + 2 child)
Fares vary on some Special Event days.
Fares allow unlimited travel on the day of issue except on Special Event days.

Detailed Directions by Car:
The Spa Valley Railway is in the southern part of Tunbridge Wells, 100 yards off the A26. Tunbridge Wells Station is adjacent to Sainsbury's and Homebase.   For Eridge Station (Satnav TN3 9LE), follow signs off the A26.

STAINMORE RAILWAY

Address: Kirby Stephen East Station, South Road, Kirkby Stephen CA17 4LA
Telephone Nº: (01768) 371700
Year Formed: 2000
Location: Kirkby Stephen
Length: One third of a mile

Nº of Steam Locos: 2
Nº of Other Locos: 3
Approx Nº of Visitors P.A.: 5,000
Gauge: Standard
Website: www.kirkbystepheneast.co.uk

GENERAL INFORMATION

Nearest Mainline Station: Kirkby Stephen (1 mile)
Car Parking: Available at the Station
Coach Parking: At the Station
Souvenir Shop(s): Yes
Food & Drinks: Light refreshments are available from an LNER Buffet car.

SPECIAL INFORMATION

Stainmore Railway is located at Kirkby Stephen East Station, the eastern terminus of the Eden Valley Railway which was closed in 1974. The site was purchased in 1997 and volunteers have since converted the derelict station to develop a Heritage Centre and operational railway which welcomes visitors at weekends.

OPERATING INFORMATION

Opening Times: Sundays from Easter until the second weekend in December, 10.00am to 4.00pm. Also open for Special Event Days on certain Saturdays: 19th April; 12th & 26th July; 16th & 23rd August and 1st November.
Steam Working: On selected days only. Please contact the railway for further information.
Prices: Adult £7.00
 Family £14.00 (2 Adults + 3 Children)
 Additional Children £1.00 each
 Concessions £5.00 to £6.00
Note: Admission to the site is free but charges apply for train rides and certain events. Santa Specials operate on dates in December and adults can also be 'Driver for a Fiver' on selected dates.

Detailed Directions by Car:
From the A66: Exit onto the A685 signposted for Brough/Kirkby Stephen and continue for 4 miles. Upon reaching Kirkby Stephen, pass through the town then turn right immediately after the Croglin Castle Pub for the railway; From the East (Tebay): Exit the M6 at Junction 38 and follow the A685 to Kirkby Stephen (approximately 10 miles). After passing Kirkby Stephen (West) Station, turn left just after crossing the bridge for the railway.

STEPHENSON STEAM RAILWAY

Address: Stephenson Railway Museum, Middle Engine Lane, North Shields, NE29 8DX
Telephone Nº: (0191) 277 7135
Year Formed: 1986
Website: info@stephensonsteamrailway.org.uk
E-mail: info@stephensonsteamrailway.org.uk

Location: Stephenson Railway Museum
Length of Line: 1½ miles
Nº of Steam Locos: 5
Nº of Other Locos: 2
Approx Nº of Visitors P.A.: 46,000
Gauge: Standard

GENERAL INFORMATION

Nearest Mainline Station: Newcastle Central (5 miles) or for the Metro Percy Main (1½ miles)
Nearest Bus Station: North Shields
Car Parking: Free parking available on site
Coach Parking: Free parking available on site
Souvenir Shop(s): Yes

SPECIAL INFORMATION

The exhibits include the engine 'Billy' which is believed to have been built at Killingworth Colliery's Workshops under the supervision of George Stephenson in 1816!

OPERATING INFORMATION

Opening Times: 2025 dates: Most Sundays and Bank Holidays from 5th April to 26th October and also on Thursdays during the School Holidays. Open from 11.00am to 4.00pm.
Steam Working: Sundays and Bank Holiday Mondays from June to September.
Prices: Adult Day Rover £8.00
Concessionary Day Rover £6.00
A voluntary donation of £1.00 can be added to the cost of tickets.
Note: Admission to the museum itself is free of charge. Season Tickets are also available and the Under-5s ride free of charge.

Detailed Directions by Car:
The Railway is adjacent to the Silverlink Retail Park approximately ½ mile from the junction between the A19 and A1058. From the A19/A1058 junction look for the signs for 'Silverlink' before following the Brown tourist signs to the Stephenson Railway Museum.

THE STRATHSPEY RAILWAY

Address: Aviemore Station, Dalfaber Road, Aviemore   PH22 1PY
Telephone Nº: (01479) 810725
Year Formed: 1971
Location of Line: Aviemore to Boat of Garten and Broomhill, Inverness-shire
Length of Line: 9½ miles at present

Nº of Steam Locos: 7 (2 in service)
Nº of Other Locos: 10
Approx Nº of Visitors P.A.: 81,000
Gauge: Standard
Website: www.strathspeyrailway.co.uk
E-mail: enquiries@strathspeyrailway.co.uk

GENERAL INFORMATION

Nearest Mainline Station: Aviemore – Strathspey trains depart from Platform 3
Nearest Bus Station: Aviemore (adjacent)
Car Parking: Available at all stations
Coach Parking: Available at Aviemore and Broomhill stations
Souvenir Shop(s): Yes – at all stations
Food & Drinks: Available on most services

SPECIAL INFORMATION

Experience the stunning Scottish Highlands in a way like no other as the Railway wends its way through the stunning Cairngorm Mountains.

OPERATING INFORMATION

Opening Times: 2025 dates: Weekends, Bank Holidays, Wednesdays and Thursdays from April to October. Also open on Fridays from 6th June to 26th September and Tuesdays in July and August. Generally open from 10.30am to 4.30pm.
Steam Working: Most trains are steam-hauled but special diesel services are timetabled throughout the year. Please check the website for further details.
Prices: Adult Return £24.50
    Child Return £14.50 (Under-5s ride free)
    Concession Return £22.50
    Family Return £55.00

Detailed Directions by Car:
For Aviemore Station from South: Take the A9 then B970 and turn left between the railway & river bridges. For Boat of Garten from North; Take the A9 then A938 to Carr Bridge, then B9153 and A95 and follow the signs; From North East: Take A95 to Boat of Garten or Broomhill (3½ miles South from Grantown-on-Spey.

Swanage Railway

Address: Station House, Railway Station Approach, Swanage, Dorset BH19 1HB
Telephone Nº: (01929) 425800
Year Formed: 1976
Location of Line: Swanage to Norden
Length of Line: 6 miles

Nº of Steam Locos: 8 (3 in service)
Nº of Other Locos: 6
Gauge: Standard
Approx Nº of Visitors P.A.: 216,000
Website: www.swanagerailway.co.uk
E-mail: info@swanagerailway.co.uk

GENERAL INFORMATION

Nearest Mainline Station: Wareham (10 miles)
Nearest Bus Station: Swanage Station (adjacent)
Car Parking: Park & Ride at Norden. Public car parks in Swanage (5 minutes walk)
Coach Parking: Available at Norden
Souvenir Shop(s): Yes – at Swanage Station
Food & Drinks: Yes – buffet available on trains and also Swanage Station Buffet and at Norden.

SPECIAL INFORMATION

The railway runs along part of the route of the old Swanage to Wareham railway, opened in 1885.

OPERATING INFORMATION

Opening Times: 2025 dates: Daily from 28th March to 2nd November but closed on Mondays and Fridays in April, September and October. Also open on a number of other dates throughout the year including Santa Specials in December. Evening services operate during some dates in the school summer holidays.
Steam Working: Most services are steam-hauled. Please check the website for further details.
Prices: Adult Day Rover £32.50
Child Day Rover £16.25 (Under-5s free)
Note: Prices shown above are for Freedom of the Line for the day tickets but lower prices apply for shorter journeys, family tickets bookings made in advance.

Detailed Directions by Car:
Norden Park & Ride Station is situated off the A351 on the approach to Corfe Castle. Swanage Station is situated in the centre of the town, just a few minutes walk from the beach. Take the A351 to reach Swanage.

SWINDON & CRICKLADE RAILWAY

Address: Blunsdon Station, Tadpole Lane, Blunsdon, Swindon, Wilts SN25 2DA
Phone Nº: (01793) 771615
Year Formed: 1978
Web: www.swindon-cricklade-railway.org
E-mail: publicity@swindon-cricklade-railway.org
Location: Mouldon Hill to Hayes Knoll
Length of Line: 2½ miles
Nº of Steam Locos: 6   **Other Locos:** 9
Approx Nº of Visitors P.A.: 16,000
Gauge: Standard

Photo by Pete Todd

GENERAL INFORMATION
Nearest Mainline Station: Swindon (5 miles)
Nearest Bus Station: Bus stop at Oakhurst (¾ mile)
Car Parking: Free parking at Blunsdon Station
Coach Parking: Free parking at Blunsdon Station
Souvenir Shop(s): Yes
Food & Drinks: Yes

SPECIAL INFORMATION
The Engine Shed at Hayes Knoll Station is occasionally open to the public.

OPERATING INFORMATION
Opening Times: 2025 dates: The Railway is open most weekends and on Bank Holidays from 29th March to 26th October. Santa Specials run in December and various other Special Events throughout the year also have Steam train rides. Open 10.30am to 4.00pm.
Steam Working: Most Sundays – please contact the railway for further details.
Prices: Adult £10.00
　　　　　Child £8.00 (Under-3s ride free)
　　　　　Concessions £9.00
Note: Prices are different on Special Event days.

Detailed Directions by Car:
From the M4: Exit the M4 at Junction 15 and follow the A419. Turn left towards Blunsdon Stadium and follow the signs for the Railway: From Cirencester: Follow the A419 to the top of Blunsdon Hill, then turn right and follow signs for Blundson Stadium.

TANFIELD RAILWAY

Address: Marley Hill Engine Shed,
Old Marley Hill, Gateshead, Tyne & Wear
NE16 5ET
Telephone Nº: 0750 809-2365
Year Formed: 1976
Location of Line: Between Sunniside & East Tanfield, Co. Durham
Length of Line: 3 miles

Nº of Steam Locos: 29 Standard, 2 Narrow
Nº Other Locos: 12 Standard, 15 Narrow
Approx Nº of Visitors P.A.: 40,000
Gauge: Standard and Narrow gauge
Website: www.tanfield-railway.co.uk
E-mail: info@tanfield-railway.co.uk

GENERAL INFORMATION

Nearest Mainline Station: Newcastle-upon-Tyne (8 miles)
Nearest Bus St'n: Gateshead Interchange (6 miles)
Car Parking: Spaces for 150 cars at Andrews House and 100 spaces at East Tanfield
Coach Parking: Spaces for 6 or 7 coaches only
Souvenir Shop(s): Yes
Food & Drinks: Yes – light snacks only

SPECIAL INFORMATION

Tanfield Railway is the oldest existing railway in use – it was originally opened in 1725. It also runs beside The Causey Arch, the oldest railway bridge in the world.

OPERATING INFORMATION

Opening Times: 2025 dates: Most Sundays and Bank Holiday Mondays from 2nd March to 12th October and most Saturdays from 19th July to 30th August. Santa Specials run on weekends and some other dates during November and December.
Steam Working: Most trains are steam-hauled and run from 10.30am to 3.30pm (from 10.30am to 3.00pm during the Winter months).
Prices: Adult £17.00
Child £5.00 (Under-5's travel free)
Concessions £15.00
Note: Special Event days may have higher prices and tickets booked online are cheaper.

Detailed Directions by Car:
Sunniside Station is off the A6076 Sunniside to Stanley road in Co. Durham. To reach the Railway, leave A1(M), follow signs for Beamish museum at Chester-le-Street then continue to Stanley and follow Tanfield Railway signs.

TELFORD STEAM RAILWAY

Address: The Old Loco Shed, Bridge Road, Horsehay, Telford, Shropshire TF4 3UH
Telephone Enquiries: (01952) 503880
Year Formed: 1976
Location: Horsehay & Dawley Station
Length of Line: 1 mile standard gauge, an eighth of a mile 2 foot narrow gauge

N° of Steam Locos: 5 (2 operational)
N° of Other Locos: 11
Approx N° of Visitors P.A.: 10,000
Website: www.telfordsteamrailway.co.uk
E-mail: enquiries@telfordsteamrailway.co.uk

GENERAL INFORMATION

Nearest Mainline Station: Wellington or Telford Central
Nearest Bus Station: Dawley (1 mile)
Car Parking: Free parking at the site
Coach Parking: Free parking at the site
Souvenir Shop(s): 'Freight Stop Gift Shop'
Food & Drinks: 'The Furnaces' Tea Room

SPECIAL INFORMATION

Telford Steam Railway has both a Standard Gauge and Narrow Gauge line as well as Miniature and Model Railways. A major extension to the line has recently opened.

OPERATING INFORMATION

Opening Times: 2025 dates: Sundays and Bank Holiday Mondays between 20th April and 28th September. Polar Express rides operate on dates during December. Open 10.30am to 4.30pm.
Steam Working: Most Bank Holidays.
Please contact the railway for further information.
Prices: Adult all day tickets £10.00
Child all day tickets £7.00
Family all day tickets £28.00
(2 adults + 2 children)
Note: Higher prices apply for Special Event days and season tickets are available.

Detailed Directions by Car:
From All Parts: Exit the M54 at Junction 6, travel south along the A5223 then follow the brown tourist signs for the railway. Note: If using a SatNav please enter TF4 2NF as the destination postcode.

Tyseley Locomotive Works Visitor Centre

Address: 670 Warwick Road, Tyseley, Birmingham B11 2HL
Telephone Nº: (0121) 708-4960
Year Formed: 1969
Location of Museum: Tyseley
Length of Line: One third of a mile

Nº of Steam Locos: Varies with visiting Locos and restoration contracts
Approx Nº of Visitors P.A.: 10,000+
Gauge: Standard
Website: www.vintagetrains.co.uk

GENERAL INFORMATION
Nearest Mainline Station: Tyseley (5 mins. walk)
Car Parking: 200 spaces at Railway site
Coach Parking: Space at Railway site
Souvenir Shop(s): Yes
Food & Drinks: None

SPECIAL INFORMATION
Originally opened in 1908, this GWR locomotive depot houses the Country's biggest collection of Mainline operating steam locos and is also the base for the Shakespeare Express plus other steam excursions which run on the Mainline. Details of all of these can be found on the centre's website.

OPERATING INFORMATION
Opening Times: Please check the website for details of how to book a Guided Depot Tour, for further information about Depot Opening Days or for details of the various Mainline services which are operated by the Vintage Trains operating company.
Steam Working: On all open days.
Guided Tour prices:
  Adults £12.00
  Children £6.00
Note: As the tour is unsuitable for younger children bookings can only be accepted for children aged 10 years or above.

Detailed Directions by Car:
From the North: Exit the M6 at Junction 6 and take A41 ring road towards Solihull; From the South: Exit the M42 at Junction 5 and take the A41 towards Birmingham.

THE WEARDALE RAILWAY

Address: Stanhope Station, Stanhope, Bishop Auckland   DL13 2YS
Telephone Nº: 07729 765504
Year Formed: 1993
Website: www.weardale-railway.org.uk
E-mail: weardalerailway@aucklandproject.org

Location: Stanhope to Bishop Auckland
Length of Line: 18 miles
Nº of Steam Locos: 1
Nº of Other Locos: 4 (including DMUs)
Gauge: Standard

GENERAL INFORMATION

Nearest Mainline Station: Bishop Auckland (¼ mile)
Nearest Bus Station: Bishop Auckland
Car Parking: Available at both Stanhope and Wolsingham Stations
Coach Parking: Available at Wolsingham Station
Souvenir Shop(s): Yes
Food & Drinks: Yes – Signal Box Cafe, Stanhope

SPECIAL INFORMATION

Weardale is in the heart of the North Pennines and the railway provides magnificent unspoilt views. The area is known for its footpaths and bridleways and the railway provides a useful base for walks between stations along banks of the beautiful River Wear.

OPERATING INFORMATION

Opening Times: 2025 heritage rail services will operate most Saturdays and Wednesdays from 16th April to 30th August, plus Sundays in August. For details of September services, please check the website for further information when planning a visit.
Trains run from 10.45am to 3.45pm.
Steam Working: None at present.
Prices: Adult Day Rover £16.00
   Child Day Rover £8.00 (Under-5s free)
   Concession Day Rover £14.00
   Family Day Rover £41.00
   (2 adult + 3 child)
Note: Prices shown are for Day Rover journeys from Stanhope to Bishop Auckland. Lower prices are charged for travel between Stanhope and Wolsingham.

Detailed Directions by Car:
From All Parts: Stanhope Station is located in Stanhope, just off the A689; Bishop Auckland West Station is a short walk from the Northern Rail Mainline Station in Bishop Auckland (SatNavs use DL14 7TL).

WENSLEYDALE RAILWAY

Address: Leeming Bar Station, Leases Road, Leeming Bar, Northallerton   DL7 9AR
Telephone Nº: (01677) 425805
Year Formed: The railway association was formed in 1990, the Railway PLC in 2000.
Location of Line: Leeming Bar to Redmire
Length of Line: Approximately 16 miles

Nº of Steam Locos: None at present
Nº of Other Locos: 10 + 2 DMUs
Approx Nº of Visitors P.A.: Not known
Gauge: Standard
Website: www.wensleydalerail.com
E-mail: admin@wensleydalerail.com

GENERAL INFORMATION

Nearest Mainline Station: Northallerton (7 miles)
Nearest Bus Station: Northallerton (7 miles)
Car & Coach Parking: Available at Leeming Bar, Leyburn and Redmire Stations
Souvenir Shop(s): Yes
Food & Drinks: At Leeming Bar, Bedale & Leyburn stations.

SPECIAL INFORMATION

Most services are operated via DMU and travel to Leyburn & Redmire tourist destinations but Heritage Diesel journeys are also available.

OPERATING INFORMATION

Opening Times: 2025 dates: Weekends and Bank Holidays from 16th February to 19th October. Also open on Wednesdays from 2nd April to 24th September plus Tuesdays and Fridays from 3rd June to 29th August. Details of other Event Days including Polar Express Rides in November and December will appear on the website.
Steam Working: None at present.
Prices: A variety of single and Day Ticket fares are available for both standard DMU and Heritage Diesel services.

Detailed Directions by Car:
From All Parts: Exit the A1 at the Leeming Bar exit and take the A684 towards Northallerton. The station is on the left after about ¼ mile close to the road junction and after the traffic lights.   By Bus: The Dales & District 73 bus route travels between Northallerton and Leeming Bar.

WEST SOMERSET RAILWAY

Address: The Railway Station, Minehead, Somerset   TA24 5BG
Telephone Nº: (01643) 704996 (enquiries)
Year Formed: 1976
Website: www.west-somerset-railway.co.uk
E-mail: info@wsrail.net

Location: Bishops Lydeard to Minehead
Length of Line: 19¾ miles
Nº of Steam Locos: 6
Nº of Other Locos: 9
Approx Nº of Visitors P.A.: 200,000
Gauge: Standard

GENERAL INFORMATION

Nearest Mainline Station: Taunton (4 miles)
Nearest Bus Station: Taunton (4½ miles) – Service 28 run to Bishops Lydeard, Watchet, Washford and Minehead.
Car Parking: Available at all stations except Doniford Halt. Free parking at Bishops Lydeard.
Coach Parking: As above
Souvenir Shops: Yes – at Minehead, Bishops Lydeard and Washford. Sales counters at other stations.
Food & Drinks: Yes – At some stations. Buffet cars on most trains.

SPECIAL INFORMATION

Britain's longest Standard gauge Heritage railway runs through the Quantock Hills and along the Bristol Channel Coast. The line passes through no fewer than ten Stations with museums at Washford and Blue Anchor and a turntable at Minehead.

OPERATING INFORMATION

Opening Times: 2025 dates: Most days from 29th March to 2nd November except some Mondays, Fridays and Thursdays. Santa Specials run on weekends and other dates from 29th November to 31st December. Open 10.00am to 5.00pm. Please check the website for further details.
Steam Working: All operating days except during Diesel Galas.
Prices: Adult Day Rover £35.00
              Child Day Rover £17.50 (Ages 5 to 15)
              Family Rover £87.50 (2 adult + 2 child)
Note: Prices shown are for tickets bought on the day of travel but advance bookings are cheaper.

Detailed Directions by Car:
Exit the M5 at Taunton (Junction 25) and follow the A358 towards Minehead. Bishops Lydeard Station is signposted from the village bypass. The A39 (which the A358 joins at Williton) goes directly past Washford Station. Minehead Station is on the seafront at the edge of the town centre, approximately ½ miles from Butlins Holiday Centre.

WHITWELL & REEPHAM RAILWAY

Address: Whitwell Road, Reepham, Norfolk   NR10 4GA
Telephone Nº: (01603) 871694
Year Formed: 2009
Location of Line: Norfolk
Length of Line: 1 mile

Nº of Steam Locos: 2
Nº of Other Locos: 4
Approx Nº of Visitors P.A.: 20,000
Gauge: Standard
Website: www.whitwellstation.com
E-mail: info@whitwellstation.com

GENERAL INFORMATION

Nearest Mainline Station: Norwich (15 miles)
Nearest Bus Station: Norwich (15 miles)
Car Parking: Available on site
Coach Parking: Available
Souvenir Shop(s): Yes
Food & Drinks: Available in 'The Sidings' café bar

SPECIAL INFORMATION

The Society was formed in 2009 and has restored the station, relaid track and sidings and acquired more rolling stock.
The station itself has been preserved as a museum, ticket office and shop with a further museum, 7¼ inch miniature railway and 'The Sidings' a purpose-built café, bar and function room also on site.

OPERATING INFORMATION

Opening Times: Open for static viewing daily (except Mondays) throughout the year from 10.00am until 4.00pm. Diesel services run at weekends throughout the year except when Steam trains are running.
Please check the railway's website for further details.
Steam Working: The first Sunday of each month plus a number of other Special Event days.
Please contact the railway for further details.
Steam services operate from 12.30pm to 4.00pm.
Prices: Adult £5.00
            Child £3.00
Note: Prices shown above are for train rides – admission to the museum is free except during the Steam Rally held in the first week in August.

Detailed Directions by Car:
From All Parts: Take the A1067 Norwich to Fakenham Road to Bawdeswell then follow the B1145 to Reepham. The railway is located about 1 mile to the South-west of Reepham and is well-signposted.

Yeovil Railway Centre

Address: Yeovil Junction Station, Stoford, Yeovil BA22 9UU
Telephone Nº: (01935) 410420
Year Formed: 1993
Location of Line: Yeovil Junction
Length of Line: ¼ mile
Gauge: Standard

Nº of Steam Locos: 2
Nº of Other Locos: 3
Approx Nº of Visitors P.A.: 5,000
Website: www.yeovilrailway.freeservers.com
E-mail: yeovilrailway@hotmail.com

GENERAL INFORMATION

Nearest Mainline Station: Yeovil Junction (adjacent)
Nearest Bus Station: Yeovil Bus Station (2 miles)
Car Parking: Available on site
Coach Parking: Available nearby
Souvenir Shop(s): Yes
Food & Drinks: Available

SPECIAL INFORMATION

The Visitor Centre is located in a GWR Transfer Shed which was built in 1864. The centre also runs Driver Experience days and their Peckett steam engine 'Pectin' returned to service in 2019.

OPERATING INFORMATION

Opening Times: 2025 Dates: 16th & 30th March; 6th, 20th, 21st & 27th April; 4th, 11th, 24th & 25th May; 1st, 15th & 29th June; 6th, 9th, 13th, 26th & 27th July; 5th, 10th, 12th, 16th, 19th, 24th & 26th August; 7th, 14th, 27th & 28th September; 25th & 31st October. Open for static viewing every Sunday morning from 10.00am until noon. Santa Specials run on 6th, 13th, 14th, 20th, 21st & 23rd December but must be pre-booked.
Steam Working: Please check website for details.
Prices: Adult £12.50
                Child £6.00 (Ages 5 to 15)
Note: Prices shown above are for Steam Working days.

Detailed Directions by Car:
The Centre is part of Yeovil Junction Station which is served by South Western Railway. By road simply follow the signs to Yeovil Junction Station from Yeovil town centre or from the A37 Dorchester to Yeovil road. The entrance to Yeovil Railway Centre is through the low bridge, half way up the Yeovil Junction Station approach road.

YORKSHIRE WOLDS RAILWAY

Address: Beverley Road, Fimber, Driffield   YO25 3HG
Telephone Nº: (01377) 338053
Year Formed: 2008
Location: Near Wetwang off the A166 York to Driffield Road.
Length: ¼ mile at present

Nº of Steam Locos: None
Nº of Other Locos: 1
Approx Nº of Visitors P.A.: not known
Gauge: Standard
Web: www.yorkshirewoldsrailway.org.uk
E-mail: info@yorkshirewoldsrailway.org.uk

GENERAL INFORMATION

Nearest Mainline Station: Driffield (9 miles)
Nearest Bus Station: Wetwang (2 miles)
Car Parking: Free parking available at the Station
Coach Parking: At the Station
Souvenir Shop(s): Yes
Food & Drinks: Light refreshments are available

SPECIAL INFORMATION

The railway operates on a small section of the former Malton & Driffield Junction Railway which opened in 1853 and was closed in 1958.

The railway has a visitor centre and offers Brake Van rides behind their locomotive, 'Sir Tatton Sykes'. Planning permission is in place to extend the line by 1 mile to Wetwang Green Lane.

OPERATING INFORMATION

Opening Times: 2025: Sundays and Bank Holidays from Easter to 26th October and also on Wednesdays during August.
Steam Working: None at present
Prices: All train rides are £5.00 per person or £12.50 per family. Full Day Passes are also available.

Detailed Directions by Car:
From York: Take the A166 eastwards towards Wetwang and, after approximately 25 miles, turn left onto the B1248 (signposted Malton). The station is on the right after approximately ¾ mile; From the South: Exit the M62 at Junction 37 and follow the A614 for approximately 22 miles. After passing through Bainton, take the 2nd exit onto the B1248 and continue northwards to Wetwang. Turn left onto the A166 and, after passing through Wetwang, turn right onto the B1248 (signposted Malton). The station is on the right after approximately ¾ mile.

NATIONAL RAILWAY MUSEUM – YORK

Address: National Railway Museum, Leeman Road, York YO26 4XJ
Telephone Nº: 033 0058 0058
Year Formed: 1975
Location of Line: York
Length of Line: Short demonstration line

Nº of Steam Locos: 79
Nº of Other Locos: 37
Approx Nº of Visitors P.A.: 900,000
Website: www.nrm.org.uk
E-mail: info@sciencemuseumgroup.ac.uk

GENERAL INFORMATION

Nearest Mainline Station: York (¼ mile)
Nearest Bus Station: York (¼ mile)
Car Parking: On site long stay car park
Coach Parking: On site
Souvenir Shop(s): Yes
Food & Drinks: Excellent on-site catering facilities.

SPECIAL INFORMATION

The Museum is the greatest of its kind in the world, housing the Nation's collection of locomotives. However, extensive building work to transform it into a 'global engineering powerhouse' will not be completed until 2027 so please expect possible disruption until then.

OPERATING INFORMATION

Opening Times: Open daily from 10.00am to 4.00pm, except from 24th to 26th of December.
Steam Working: None at present
Prices: Free admission but visitors are invited to make a donation and pre-booking is advised to guarantee entry.

Detailed Directions by Car:
The Museum is located in the centre of York, just behind the Railway Station. It is clearly signposted from all approaches to York and can be accessed by foot via the Station Footbridge.

LOCOMOTION

Address: Locomotion, Dale Road, Shildon   DL4 2RE
Telephone Nº: 033 0058 0058
Year Formed: 2004
Location: Shildon, County Durham
Length of Line: Over ½ mile

Nº of Steam Locos: 70+ locomotives and other rail vehicles
Approx Nº of Visitors P.A.: 200,000
Gauge: Standard
Website: www.locomotion.org.uk
E-mail: info@sciencemuseumgroup.ac.uk

GENERAL INFORMATION

Nearest Mainline Station: Shildon (adjacent)
Nearest Bus Station: Durham
Car Parking: Available on site
Coach Parking: Available on site
Souvenir Shop(s): Yes
Food & Drinks: Yes

SPECIAL INFORMATION

A Locomotion you can see highlights of the British National Collection of railway vehicles in the world's first railway town. The museum is home to more than 70 National Rail Collection vehicles, including such icons as 'Sans Pareil', 'APT-E' and the Deltic prototype.

OPERATING INFORMATION

Opening Times: 2025 dates: Open daily throughout the year except on the 25th & 26th December. The Museum opens from 10.00am to 5.00pm.
Steam Working: Special Event Days only. Please contact the museum or check the website for further details.
Prices: Admission to the Museum is free of charge but visitors are asked to consider making a voluntary donation.

Detailed Directions by Car:
From All Parts: Exit the A1(M) at Junction 58 and take the A68 and the A6072 to Shildon. Follow the Brown tourist signs to Locomotion which is situated ¼ mile to the south-east of the Town Centre.
Drivers using SATNAVs should enter the following post code: DL4 2RE

STEAM – MUSEUM OF THE GREAT WESTERN RAILWAY

Address: STEAM – Museum of the Great Western Railway, Fire Fly Avenue, Swindon SN2 2EY **Telephone Nº:** (01793) 466646 **Year Formed:** 2000	**Nº of Steam Locos:** 8 **Nº of Other Locos:** 1 **Approx Nº of Visitors P.A.:** 100,000 **Website:** www.steam-museum.org.uk **E-mail:** steammuseum@swindon.gov.uk

GENERAL INFORMATION

Nearest Mainline Station: Swindon (10 min. walk)
Nearest Bus Station: Swindon (10 minute walk)
Car Parking: Ample parking space available in the Outlet Centre (charges apply)
Coach Parking: Free parking on site and nearby
Souvenir Shop(s): Yes
Food & Drinks: There is a Café within the Museum

SPECIAL INFORMATION

STEAM tells the story of the men and women who built the Great Western Railway.

OPERATING INFORMATION

Opening Times: Open daily (except 24th to 26th December & 1st January) from 10.00am to 5.00pm (11.00am to 4.00pm on Sundays)
Last admission is 4.00pm (3.00pm on Sundays).
Steam Working: During some special events only – please check the Museum website for details.
Prices: Adult Tickets £13.80
  Child Tickets £10.20 (Under-3's free)
  Concession Tickets £11.10
  Family Tickets £30.80 to £52.40
  (prices depend on number in family)
Note: All tickets are timed and must be pre-booked.

Detailed Directions by Car:
Exit the M4 at Junction 16 and follow the brown tourist signs to 'Outlet Centre'. Similarly follow the brown signs from all other major routes. From the Railway Station: STEAM is a 10 to 15 minute walk and is accessible through the pedestrian tunnel – entrance by Emlyn Square.

Hopetown – Darlington

Address: Hopetown, McNay Street, Darlington   DL3 6SW
Telephone Nº: (01325) 405060
Year Formed: 1975 (as Head of Steam)
Location of Line: Adjacent to North Road Station
Length of Line: ¼ mile

Nº of Steam Locos: 4
Nº of Other Locos: None
Approx Nº of Visitors P.A.: 40,000
Gauge: Standard
Website: www.hopetowndarlington.co.uk
E-mail: hopetown@darlington.gov.uk

GENERAL INFORMATION

Nearest Mainline Station: North Road (adjacent)
Car Parking: Free parking at site
Coach Parking: Free parking at site
Souvenir Shop(s): Yes
Food & Drinks: Available on site

SPECIAL INFORMATION

Home to the World's first steam locomotive-hauled passenger carrying Public Railway, this 7½ acre site houses an 1833 Goods Shed, the 1842 Station, a modern locomotive construction works and many more heritage railway attractions.

OPERATING INFORMATION

Opening Times: Hopetown is open daily throughout the year but is closed every Monday (except during the School Holidays). It is also closed on Christmas Day, Boxing Day and New Year's Day. Open 10.00am to 5.00pm with the last entry at 4.00pm.
Prices: Admission is free of charge but must be pre-booked to enable the location to manage capacity safely.

Detailed Directions by Car:
From Darlington Town Centre: Follow the A167 north for about ¾ mile then turn left immediately before the Railway bridge; From A1(M): Exit at Junction 59 then follow A167 towards Darlington and turn right after passing under the Railway bridge.

Manchester Museum of Science and Industry

Address: Liverpool Road, Manchester, M3 4FP
Telephone Nº: (0161) 832-2244
Year Opened: 1983
Web: www.scienceandindustrymuseum.org.uk

Location: Central Manchester
Nº of Steam Locos: A number of locomotives are on display
Approx Nº of Visitors P.A.: –
Gauge: Standard

GENERAL INFORMATION

Nearest Mainline Station: Deansgate (10 minutes walk)
Nearest Bus Station: Metroshuttle services 1 and 3 stop on Byrom Street, just 5 minutes walk from the museum. Visit www.tfgm.com for information about this free city centre bus service.
Nearest Tram Station (Metrolink): Deansgate-Castlefield is 10 minutes walk.
Car Parking: None available at the museum
Coach Parking: None available at the museum
Souvenir Shop(s): Yes
Food & Drinks: Available in the Museum Café

SPECIAL INFORMATION

The Museum is located at the old Liverpool Road Station, a globally-important site which was the original terminus of the world's first inter-city railway. Visitors can stand in the waiting rooms used by the very first passengers on the Liverpool and Manchester Railway.

OPERATING INFORMATION

Opening Times: Open daily from 10.00am to 5.00pm except for 24th to 26th December. Please check the Museum's website for details of Special Events.
Prices: Admission is usually free of charge but visitors are invited to make donations. An entrance fee is charged for some Special Events.

Detailed Directions by Car:
The Museum is located in the centre of Manchester. As there are no parking facilities, visitors are advised to use public transport (rail, bus and tram).

WHITEHEAD RAILWAY MUSEUM

Address: Castleview Road, Whitehead, BT38 9NA
Telephone Nº: (0289) 358-6200
Year Formed: 1965
Location of Line: Whitehead, N. Ireland
Length of Line: Short Line at Museum

Nº of Steam Locos: 10
Nº of Other Locos: 6
Gauge: Irish Standard (5 foot 3 inches)
Website: www.steamtrainsireland.com
E-mail: info@steamtrainsireland.com

GENERAL INFORMATION

Nearest Mainline Station: Whitehead (½ mile)
Car Parking: Adjacent to the nearby Youth Centre
Souvenir Shop: Online purchases can be made in both Pounds and Euros.
Food & Drinks: Available

SPECIAL INFORMATION

The Railway Preservation Society of Ireland (RPSI) was formed in 1964 and the Whitehead Railway Museum has been its home since 1965. It is now a five-gallery Museum as well as the base from which the RPSI operates excursions around the Irish Railway network in both the North and the South of Ireland.

OPERATING INFORMATION

Opening Times: The Museum opens from Thursday to Saturday throughout the year and on some other Event Days.
Usual opening times are 10.00am to 2.30pm.
Steam Working: Please check the website for details
Prices: Adults £9.00
Children £6.00 (Under-3s free)
Families £25.00 (2 adults + 3 children)
Note: Details of Special Event Days and Excursions are shown on the website and Group Admission prices are cheaper.

Detailed Directions by Car:
From Belfast: Take the M2 to the M5 at Whiteabbey then follow signs for the A2 to Carrickfergus. Pass Carrickfergus Castle and the Museum is located along the nearby Castleview Road.